A Guide to Chinese Martial Arts

by Li Tianji and Du Xilian

FOREIGN LANGUAGES PRESS
BEIJING, CHINA

First Edition 1991
Second Printing 1995

ISBN 7-119-01393-9

© Foreign Languages Press, Beijing, China, 1991

Published by Foreign Languages Press
24 Baiwanzhuang Road, Beijing 100037, China
Distributed by China International Book Trading Corporation
35 Chegongzhuang Xilu, Beijing 100044, China
P.O. Box 399, Beijing, China

Printed in the People's Republic of China

Contents

CHAPTER ONE
THE ORIGINS AND HISTORICAL DEVELOPMENT OF
CHINESE *WUSHU*   1
I. The Roots of Chinese *Wushu*   1
II. *Wushu* Before the Qin and Han Dynasties   2
III. The Sui-Tang Period and Afterwards   6
IV. Current Developments of *Wushu*   9

CHAPTER TWO
THE STYLES OF CHINESE *WUSHU*   15
I. How Many Styles of Chinese Boxing?   15
II. The Eighteen Weapons   18
III. Methods of *Wushu* Practice   20
IV. The Value of Chinese *Wushu*   21
   1. A Healthy Sport   22
   2. Self-Defence Skills   24
   3. The Beauty of Chinese *Wushu*   24
   4. Virtue and Skill   25

CHAPTER THREE
AN INTRODUCTION TO SOME *WUSHU* STYLES   26
I. *Chang Quan*   26
   1. Evolution and Characteristics   26
   2. Essential Skills   28
   3. Illustrated Basic Exercises   31

1) Hand Positions	31
2) Hand Technique	32
3) Stances	38
4) Footwork	42
5) Leg Skills	45
6) Shoulder Skills	59
7) Waist Skills	60
8) Jumping	63
9) Balancing	66
10) Combined Exercise for Five Kinds of Steps	66
4. Twenty-Four Gestures of *Lianhuan Chang Quan*	74

II. *Taiji Quan* — 94

1. Origin of *Taiji Quan* — 94
2. Different Schools of *Taiji Quan* — 97
3. Practice Methods — 101
4. Basic Requirements in Practice — 102
5. *Taiji Quan* and Health — 104
6. Illustrated Simplified *Taiji Quan Exercise* — 105

III. *Shaolin Quan* — 147

1. Shaolin Monastery and Shaolin *Wushu* — 147
2. Contents and Characteristics of *Shaolin Quan* — 151
3. Illustrated *Shaolin Tiangang Quan* — 153

Chang Quan (Extended Boxing) by Li Lianjie.

Yingzhua Quan (Eagle's Talons Boxing) by Xu Xiangdong.

Tongbi Quan (Full-Arm Boxing) by Hu Baolin.

Bagua Zhang (Eight Trigram Boxing) by Ge Chunyan.

Nan Quan (Southern Boxing) by Huang Huizhen.

Fanzi Quan (Wheeling Boxing) by Chu Fenglian.

She Quan (Snake Boxing) by Zhang Xiaoyan.

Tanglang Quan (Mantis Boxing) by the nine-year-old Liu Jianhua.

Spring and Autumn Halberd.

Double-Bladed Dagger.

Twin Hooks.

Three-Sectioned Flail.

Sword and a Multi-Sectioned Whip.

Sky-Measuring Combs.

Monk's Spade.

Crescent-shaped spade.

Chapter One
The Origins and Historical Development of Chinese *Wushu*

Wushu, or martial arts, is a sport for health and self-defence, with a history of several thousand years and part of China's valuable cultural heritage.

I. The Roots of Chinese *Wushu*

Chinese *wushu* was developed through the centuries by the Chinese people in their struggle for survival. Its roots lie in primitive society, though, at that time, it was a far cry from the artistic sport that it is today.

In antiquity, man used clubs and sticks in his struggle against wild animals and in his search for food. A rudimentary skill in weaponry was developed and then the need for skill in arms was further stimulated by inter-tribal warfare. These conditions led to the gradual development of sophisticated weapons whose use required more skill, although hand-to-hand fighting was still basic to combat.

As man became more skillful in hunting and warfare, he also gradually developed dance for entertainment and relaxation. Ancient records suggest that dance was often the imitation of various animal movements, hence

Ill. 1. Butting with Horns

the Monkey Dance, the Bear Dance, the Bird Dance, and so on. The *Book of History*, refers to them as "the dances of the hundred animals."

In addition, rudimentary sports appeared, such as Dance with Shield and Battle-Axe and Butting with Horns (Ill. 1), both military training exercises. The Dance with Shield and Axe, which was a martial dance depicting battle and training troops, demonstrates the early relationship between dance and fighting skills. Butting with Horns was competitive wrestling practised by the soldiers. This sport was said to have been a training method before battle by the armies of the legendary Chiyou tribe of eastern China. The soldiers wore horns on their heads as a sign of courage, then butted each other during the contest (Ill. 1). These exercises were early forms of *wushu*.

II. *Wushu* Before the Qin and Han Dynasties

As society developed, so did *wushu*. The Shang period between the 16th and 11th centuries B.C. saw the flourishing of the Bronze Age in China, giving rise to an array of bronze weapons, such as the wave-bladed spear, dagger-axe, halberd, axe, battle-axe, broad-sword and rapier. These weapons required a corresponding development in skill wielding them.

During the Spring and Autumn and Warring States period between 770 and 221 B.C., cavalry replaced chariot-based warfare. To suit combat on horseback, modifications on weapons were made such as the shape of the blade or the length of the handle. New weapons were also invented.

According to the *Book of Zhuang Zi*, unarmed combat was a highly developed skill by the end of this period, with many methods of attack, defence, counter-attack and feints.

Fencing was also fairly common at that time. It was discussed in another section of the *Book of Zhuang Zi*. According to *The Sayings of the Confucian Family*, "Zi Lu went to see Confucius in battle-dress and, wielding his sword, began to dance."

Fencing was especially popular among the people of the states of Wu, Yue and Zhao. Competitions were frequent, but because contestants wore inadequate protection, injuries were common during the bouts. In one fencing competition in the state of Zhao, more than sixty people were killed or wounded over a period of seven days. In the state of Wu, scars on the body or face were a common sight among the people. Nevertheless, the love of fencing went unabated among women as well as men. *The Spring and Autumn Chronicles of Wu and Yue* tells the story of Chu Nü, who was given the honorary title "Daughter of Yue" by Yue's King, Gou Jian, who lived around 465 B.C., for her outstanding skill in martial arts. The story is that King Gou Jian was discussing plans to strengthen his country with his Prime Minister Fan Li, who advised him, "When leading the army into battle, victory or defeat is usually decided by the soldiers' skill in arms. I hear that in the Southern Forest lives a woman named Chu Nü, whose skill in martial arts far surpasses the ordinary. Might I suggest that Your Majesty summon her to instruct our troops." The King promptly agreed and sent a general to fetch her. When the general got to the Southern Forest, he found her picking leaves in a mulberry tree, seemingly unaware of his arrival. The general tried to test her ability by aiming a fierce blow at the branch on which she was standing. Before the blow had even struck, however, Chu Nü somersaulted off the tree and landed in front of his horse. She met the King, who was impressed not only by her thorough knowledge of fencing, but also her superb sword dance (Ill. 2).

By the Qin Dynasty (221-207 B.C.), competitions had developed stricter rules with referees, arenas and protective clothing. Among the articles unearthed in 1975 from a tomb of the Qin Dynasty in Jiangling County, Hubei Province, was a wooden comb (Ill. 3), on the back of which was painted in colour a scene depicting a wrestling competition. A streamer hangs from a stage where two men wrestle, their torsos bare, wearing breeches, belts around the waist, and shoes with upturned toes. A third man acts as a referee.

During the Han Dynasty (206 B.C.–A.D. 220) *wushu* was developed further, the element of sport and dance now becoming more apparent. Many martial dances appeared, such as the Rapier Dance, the Broad-Sword Dance, the Twin-Halberd Dance and the Battle-Axe Dance. While these dances contained elements of attack

Ill. 2. The Daughter of Yue Leaves the Southern Forest, a stone carving of the Han Dynasty showing a figure wielding a sword.

Ill. 3. A wooden comb unearthed from a Qin Dynasty tomb and decorated with a picuture of wrestling.

and defence, other postures and techniques evolved which were designed clearly for calisthenic purposes. An historical record in 108 B.C. tells how people came from as far as 300 *li* (150 km.) around the capital to see a contest.

It was tradition that every feast should have a dance performance which, by the Han time, would often take the form of a sword dance. The most famous one was the sword dance performed at the feast at the Swan-Goose Gate. The feast took place after the collapse of the Qin Dynasty, during the struggle for supremacy between the forces of Chu, led by Xiang Yu (232-202 B.C.) and the forces of Han, led by Liu Bang (247-195 B.C.). The story says that Liu Bang was invited to a feast at the Swan-Goose Gate by Xiang Yu. Xiang Yu's supporter, Xiang Zhuang, performed a sword dance with the intent of accidently killing Liu during his performance. But, a man named Fan Kuai joined the dance to protect Liu.

Unarmed combat contests were also popular during the Han Dynasty. The rapid developments in cavalry warfare of this period led to further improvements in skill using bladed weapons. *History of the Han Dynasty* records chapters on fencing, unarmed combat and archery. Unfortunately, however, these have all been lost.

III. The Sui-Tang Period and Afterwards

Fencing Dance became increasingly popular during the Sui and Tang dynasties (518-907). Among the well-known masters were the Tang poet Li Bai, General Pei Min and two women, Gongsun and Li Shi'er.

During the Tang Dynasty (618-907) a system was

inaugurated for selecting military officers by examination. Those highly skilled in *wushu* were given honorary titles such as "Fierce and Eager Knight," and "Fleet-Footed Knight." This system for selecting martial talent stimulated the practice of *wushu* all through society. As a result, *wushu* routines developed rapidly. New forms of single and group dance exercises were designed, involving swords, spears, broad-swords, halberds, cudgels and staffs. Boxing also appeared.

During the Song Dynasty (960-1279) *wushu* associations were organized among the people. There are records of archery, cross-bow, staff and wrestling societies. In the cities, every street and alley became a practice ground, with performances of horn-butting, boxing, kicking, staff and cudgel play, dances with broad-swords, spears, and archery. Traditional tales such as *Outlaws of the Marsh*, about the rebellion of peasant heroes against the corrupt Song government officials give a vivid picture of *wushu* in that period.

By the Ming Dynasty (1368-1644), *wushu* had gradually crystallized into many different schools. Theoretical works were written summarizing the development of the many styles; works such as *A New Work on the Effect of Martial Arts* (Ill. 4), *Martial Writings* and *Skills Additional to Tilling*. These works recorded the different schools of armed and unarmed combat, their development, technique, fighting methods, and the names of the movements. The author of *A New Work on the Effect of Martial Arts*, Qi Jiguang (1528-1587), was a renowned general under Emperor Jiajing (reigned 1522-1566) of the Ming Dynasty, and was highly skilled in nearly all kinds of weapons. He regarded unarmed combat as the most important aspect of *wushu*, as the foundation of all

Ill. 4. *A New Work on the Effect of Martial Arts*, written by Qi Jiguang, a renowned general of the sixteenth century.

fighting skills and the beginners' door to all other skills. Qi's soldiers became renowned throughout China for their bravery and skill in battle.

This period abounds in famous figures such as Ou Qianjin, famous for his outstanding fighting ability and *wushu* skill, and Zhang Songxi for his internal school of boxing. Zhang Songxi was still a formidable opponent and capable of breaking a stone slab with his bare hand at the age of seventy.

In the Qing Dynasty (1644-1911), secret *wushu* societies were common. This period saw the rapid development of many styles of *wushu*, as well as the appearance of such styles as *Taiji Quan* (Great-Ultimate Boxing), *Bagua Quan* (Eight-Trigram Boxing), *Xingyi Quan* (Imitation Boxing), *Baji Quan* (Eight-Ultimate Boxing) and *Tongbi Quan* (Full-Arm Boxing).

After the Revolution of 1911 which overthrew the Qing Dyansty, Dr. Sun Yat-sen (1866-1925), leader of the revolution, greatly encouraged the practice of *wushu* as a means to strengthen the body. *Wushu* was advocated by many other patriots, and as a result, many famous practitioners were brought to the attention of the public. In 1919, the internationally renowned *wushu* master, Huo Yuanjia, started the Superior *Wushu* Association, which became a model for other such associations. Sun Yat-sen wrote the inscription "Emulate the Martial Spirit" for the Superior *Wushu* Association.

After 1929, the Central Academy of Chinese Boxing was set up with branches in many regions to train promising *wushu* practitioners. There were also a number of non-governmental *wushu* organizations set up in cities and villages, such as the Association of Best *Wushu* in Shanghai and the Chinese Warriors' Association in Tianjin. They did much to preserve and develop *wushu* throughout China.

IV. Current Developments of *Wushu*

Since the founding of the People's Republic of China in 1949, the sport of *wushu* has been maintained, studied and developed, as part of China's cultural heritage, enabling it to spread nationwide.

Wushu associations have been established at all levels to promote and direct development. In order to meet the needs of the large numbers of enthusiasts, elementary *wushu* routines and simplified *Taiji Quan* for beginners have been formulated by associations. Standard routines for competition, *wushu* books, posters, films and videos, have been produced.

Special attention has been paid to collecting and assessing *wushu* material. Because of the tradition of handing down *wushu* forms from master to pupil by word of mouth and personal demonstration, literary sources and materials are scarce, and of these, most are scattered. Many contemporary masters have also already passed away, while those still alive are often elderly. Thus, those salvaging China's legacy are strongly motivated to systematize the *wushu* material.

In 1953, the First All-China National Sports Emulation Performance was held. Since then there have been regular *wushu* competitions and exhibitions. These activities promote the exchange of skills and ideas, find new talents and encourage *wushu* to flourish and develop. Regulated competitions raise the level of performance and help develop *wushu* in its many forms.

In order to assess the exercise value of *wushu*, research on various *wushu* styles has been done. Beijing Medical College studied the effects of *Chang Quan* (Extended Boxing) and *Taiji Quan* practices and the therapeutic value of *Taiji Quan* for the aged, weak and chronically ill.

Wushu has been placed on the physical education curriculum of most schools and colleges, while colleges of physical culture now offer *wushu* courses. There are *wushu* classes in many spare-time sports schools for young people, and *wushu* associations in different localities have set up coaching stations, attracting more and more enthusiasts.

Each morning, as the first rays of the sun appear, people practise *wushu* in parks and squares, by lakes, under trees, in convalescent homes, hospitals and practice rooms, indeed almost anywhere offering a little quiet and space (Ill. 5). Each bears in mind his or her own particular needs and preference. Some do bare-hand shadow boxing, some exercise alone, some in pairs

Ill. 5. Practising *wushu* in the morning.

Ill. 6. Coaching his grandson in fencing.

and some in groups. Such a myriad of forms and postures is a lively and inspiring scene (Ill. 6).

Chinese *wushu* has now spread throughout the world. Chinese *wushu* teams have visited more than fifty countries, delighting audiences everywhere. The first such team to go abroad was a group of young *wushu* practitioners who gave a demonstration at the Second National Sports Meet of Czechoslovakia in 1960. Then the group visited Burma, accompanying the late Chinese Premier Zhou Enlai. In 1974 the Chinese National *Wushu* Team and in 1980, the Beijing *Wushu* Team visited the United States. They received a warm welcome and proved very popular.

Many foreigners have been eager to come to China to learn *wushu*. Every year, clubs and *wushu* schools and coaching stations, as well as colleges of physical culture in many parts of China are visited by large groups of overseas *wushu* fans wishing to learn (Ill. 7). Since 1975, the Beijing International Club has organized thirty *Taiji Quan* classes attended by more than a thousand foreigners residing in China. Between 1979 and mid-1982, more than eighty foreigners attended the Beijing Institute of Physical Culture to study *wushu*, the oldest among them more than seventy years old and the youngest not yet twenty. More than half of them were women. They came mostly from Japan, Britain, the United States, Canada, Sweden, and other countries. Some were overseas Chinese.

In September 1982, the First China International *Wushu* Friendship Demonstration Contest was held in Nanjing, jointly sponsored by the Jiangsu Provincial *Wushu* Institute and the U.S. National Chinese *Wushu* Association. This was a new experiment, bringing con-

Ill. 8. Ping Lin of the American Team performing a free-style *wushu* routine at the first China International *Wushu* Friendship Demenstration Contest held in 1982.

Ill. 9. Endo Kiyohiko of the Japanese team performing *Taiji Quan* of the Chen style at the Demonstration Contest.

testants from many countries together in one arena to exchange skills (Ill. 8).

All this is evidence of a budding *wushu* craze sweeping many countries. Enthusiasts in the United States, Canada and Mexico have organizations teaching Chinese *wushu*. In 1981, Sweden, Italy, France, Britain, West Germany and Spain established the Six-Nation Kung Fu League. A *kung fu* school and *kung fu* club have been set up in Stockholm. National Chinese boxing competitions held in the Phillipines and Singapore included combat competitions according to weight class, as well as performances of *wushu* routines. *Wushu* activities have also developed rapidly in Japan, itself with a long tradition of martial arts. The Shaolin Boxing League has more than one million members, with many branches both at home and abroad. *Taiji Quan* has also spread quickly across Japan (Ill. 9).

All this is in sharp contrast to old China when the Chinese people were considered the "sick men of East Asia" and *wushu* practitioners faced discrimination. Now it is expected that Chinese *wushu* will continue to grow in popularity and spread, promoting health among all peoples, and strengthening their ties.

Ill. 7 Foreigners practising *wushu* at Beijing's International Club.

Chapter Two
The Styles of Chinese *Wushu*

I. How Many Styles of Chinese Boxing?

It is difficult to accurately assess just how many styles are practised today across China. There are more than 100 schools and many individual styles within each of these schools.

Yongchun Quan (Eternal Youth Boxing) originated in Fujian Province, later spreading south to Guangdong, Macao and Hong Kong. *Yongchun Quan* is just one of a number of styles under the general term, *Nan Quan*, the Southern School of Boxing, a vigourous and aggressive school popular south of the Yangtze River. Of the many styles of *Nan Quan*, the most well-known are *Hongjia Quan* (Hong School of Boxing), *Liujia Quan* (Liu School of Boxing), *Caijia Quan* (Cai School of Boxing), *Lijia Quan* (Li School of Boxing), and *Mojia Quan* (Mo school of Boxing), "the Five Great Schools." Other schools of *Nan Quan* are: *Huheshuangxing Quan* (Tiger and Crane Boxing), *Yongchun Quan* (Eternal Youth Boxing), *Xia Quan* (Knight Boxing), *Hakka Quan* (Hakka Boxing), *Fojia Quan* (Buddhist Boxing), *Baimei Quan* (White-Eyebrow Boxing), *Ru Quan* (Confucian Boxing), *Nanji Quan* (Southern Skills Boxing), *Kunlun Quan* (Kunlun Boxing), *Kongmen Quan* (House of Kong Boxing), *Lian-*

shou Quan (Han-Exercising Boxing), *Diaojia Jiao* (Diao School of Teaching), *Yuejia Jiao* (Yue School of Teaching) and *Songjia Jiao* (Song School of Teaching).

This large group of schools covers wide variety of styles. To take the province of Guangdong as an example, there are more than 350 different bare-hand routines, and over 100 armed routines, belonging to different schools.

Bei Quan, the Northern School of Boxing is a generic term for those schools in the provinces north of the Yangtze River. Characterized by speed and strength, the Northern School emphasizes variations of kicking and footwork, hence the common saying "Southern fists, Northern legs." The major styles of the Northern School are: *Shaolin Quan* (Shaolin Boxing), *Fanzi Quan* (Wheeling Boxing), *Zha Quan* (Zha School of Boxing), *Hwa Quan* (Essence Boxing), *Hua Quan* (Flower Boxing), *Pao Quan* (Cannon Boxing), *Hong Quan* (Hong School of Boxing), *Tongbi Quan* (Full-Arm Boxing), *Mizong Quan* (Maze Boxing), *Liuhe Quan* (Six-Harmony Boxing), *Tantui* (Springing Legs), *Chuojiao* (Jabbing Feet), *Baji Quan* (Eight-Ultimate Boxing), *Taizu Chang Quan* (Great Ancestor Extended Boxing) and *Mian Quan* (Silk Floss Boxing).

There are also the popular *Taiji Quan* and *Chang Quan*, the energetic *Xingyi Quan* (Imitation Boxing), the flowing *Bagua Quan*, the vivid *Hou Quan* (Monkey Boxing) and *Zui Quan* (Drunken Boxing), the acrobatic *Ditang Quan* (Tumbling Boxing), and more. Each has its own characteristic skills.

This myriad of forms is the result of the major schools evolving into regional styles according to developments by individual masters. Some styles have simple routines with basic skills and exercises for beginners as well as other more complicated rountines for experienced practitioners. For instance, *Taiji Quan* is divided into five major schools—the Yang, Chen, Wu, Woo, and Sun. These schools further include a variety of forms. For instance, the Chen school includes an Old routine, a New routine, and the Zhaobao routine. The Yang school includes the Greater routine and the Lesser routine.

With so many categories, schools and styles, there is a clear need for systematization in order to organize competitions, and promote *wushu*. In competitions today styles come under seven catagories.

1. The free-style *Chang Quan* Group—These are routines devised since the founding of New China. Based on the traditional *Chang Quan* school, these routines consist of fixed postures with unified standards and teaching material. Characterized by expansive and agile movements, they are suitable for children.

2. The *Taiji Quan* Group—Including all the traditional and new styles. Suitable for most people, these postures are useful in treating illness and strengthening the constitution.

3. The *Nan Quan* Group—The movements of these southern styles are powerful and energetic, with variations of striking methods by the arms, and explosive shouts accompanying the movement.

4. The *Xingyi-Bagua* Group—Characterized by stable, well-rooted movements and simple forms. Movements are led with the mind, emphasizing the inner and outer unity of mind, form and strength.

5. The *Tongbi-Pigua* Group—Styles characterized by open and ample movements, striking far and long, bearing down on the opponent in fast, concentrated

bursts.

6. The Imitation-*Ditang* Group—A vivid, lively style with much leaping and rolling in imitation of various animals.

7. The miscellaneous group—Incorporating the various traditional northern styles. They are fast, with agile, fluctuating movements, interweaving motion and stillness, and short and long thrusts.

II. The Eighteen Weapons

As already mentioned, Chinese *wushu* involves practice with weapons as well as the standard bare-hand skills. The majority of these weapons have been adapted from traditional weapons, hence the use of the term the "eighteen military weapons." This term was already widely used during the Song Dynasty (960-1279). The Ming novel, *Outlaws of the Marsh* mentioned it frequently. One version of the book records the "eighteen military weapons" as the lance, mallet, long bow, crossbow, jingal, jointed bludgeon, truncheon, sword, chain, hooks, hatchet, dagger-axe, battle-axe, halberd, shield, staff, spear and rake.

To which weapons the term "eighteen weapons" referred varied according to the historical period and the school of *wushu* involved. Today, the term generally refers to the broad-sword, lance, rapier, halberd, hatchet, battle-axe, shovel, fork, jointed bludgeon, truncheon, hammer, harrow, trident, staff, long-blade spear, cudgel, dagger-axe and wave-bladed spear.

This is only a general term, since military weapons were never restricted to just eighteen forms. Other weapons frequently used include the rope-dart, Emei dagger named after the Emei Mountain in Sichuan Province from which the style originated, as well as the bent-handled club and hook. Each category also encompasses many items. For instance, the broad-sword category includes the long-handled broad-sword, the short-handled broad-sword, single broad-sword, double broad-swords, and the three pointed, two-edged broad-sword. The staffs consist of the long staff, eye-brow level staff, short staff, long-handled flail, short-handled flail and three-sectioned flail.

Each weapon requires special skills to use. According to *wushu* classics, "Lance thrusts along a line, staff strikes in a great slice and the broad-sword is like a ferocious tiger, the rapier like a roving dragon."

Each style often has its own method for wielding a weapon. The staff, for instance, no matter which style is practised, advocates the thrust, slash, sweep, and spin for long assaults, and the jab, stir, prod and the upward thrust for close-quarter combat. However, the single-head staff used by *Nan Quan* styles emphasizes power rather than flourish, while the eye-brow level staff of *Chang Quan* is full of twirls and flourishes.

Today, the wide variety of weapons used in *wushu* practice fall into four groups:

1. Long Weapons: Longer than the height of a person and wielded with both hands during practice. They include the lance, staff, great broad-sword, spear, halberd, fork, trident and spade.

2. Short Weapons: Shorter than the height of a person and wielded with one hand. These include the broad-sword, rapier, hatchet, hammer, truncheon, jointed bludgeon, dagger and shield.

3. Soft weapons: Rope, chains, or rings are used to create linked weapons which are able to strike close or far and are wielded with one or both hands. They include the nine-sectioned chain, three-sectioned flail, flying hammers which is two iron balls linked by a long iron chain, the rope dart, flying claw and the ordinary flail.

4. Twin weapons: Here a pair of weapons are wielded, one in each hand. These include twin broad-swords, twin rapiers, twin hooks, twin bludgeons, twin bent-handled clubs, twin lances, twin hatchets, twin daggers, double-bladed daggers, *Panguanbi* (Twin rods with fist-shaped heads) and duck and drake battle-axes.

III. Methods of *Wushu* Practice

There are many forms of Chinese *wushu* practice. The main three are: practice routines, combat duels, and skill-developing exercises.

Wushu routines consist of complete sets of forms, linking a continuous stream of movements, sometimes as many as one hundred. The composition, order and rhythm differ for each routine, with variations in the intensity and technical difficulty of the excercise. These practice routines can be individual bare-handed routines; individual armed routines; set duel routines involving mock combat performed by two or three persons either unarmed, armed or mixed; and group routines, bare-handed or with weapons, performed in unison by four or more persons.

Combat duels are combat practice by two contestants. Its commonest forms are:

1. Free-Style Combat—Competitions involving unarmed duels, where the aim is to knock the opponent over with kicks or punches. Competitors may or may not wear protection.

2. Push Hands—A bare-hand competition, where the competitors maintain constant contact at the wrists and aim to dislodge their opponent by pulling or pushing. No kicking, punching or wrestling is allowed.

3. Short-Cudgel Duel—Each competitor wields a short cudgel wrapped in leather or cotton padding. Both wear protection and he or she who hits the opponent wins.

4. Long-Cudgel Duel—Each competitor wields a specially made long cudgel or pole and wears protective gear. The first to hit the opponent is the winner.

Skill-developing exercises are part of the basic *wushu* training for improving strength and fundamental techniques. These include standing-pole exercise in which the trainee maintains a posture for a length of time and foot-work, kicking, stretching and tumbling. Some also involve the use of apparatus, such as punchbags and multi-layered paper for striking practice, shaking rods, and wooden poles.

IV. The Value of Chinese *Wushu*

One of the features of Chinese *wushu* is that throughout its long history it has constantly developed because it is a unique combination of healthy excercise, practical self-defence, self-discipline and art.

1. A Healthy Sport

Over 100 years ago, a *Taiji Quan* master wrote in his work entitled *Song of the Thirteen Postures*:

> Think now carefully of the purpose of
> these postures—to attain longevity
> and remain young forever.

This reflects one of the fundamental aims of Chinese *wushu*. Throughout its development, *wushu* has been part of the search for health in youth and in old age.

A set of *wushu* exercises incorporates stillness and movement, turning, and many other movements requiring different skills. Its fast and powerful strikes and agile leaps demand speed, adaptability and stamina. At the same time, the need for concentration and determination stimulates the mind and spirit.

The Beijing Institute of Physical Culture did a comparative experiment on the cardio-vascular response of a group of university students who regularly practised *wushu* and a second group of students who did not. Each student was asked to squat down 20 times in 30 seconds, with the following results:

		Increase in Pulse Rate	Increase in Systolic Pressure
Wushu practitioners:	Male	53.57%	13.85%
	Female	59.86%	15.53%
Ordinary students:	Male	61.21%	19%
	Female	63.48%	20.15%

The above experiment demonstrates that *wushu* can improve the performance of the cardio-vascular system, lowering the pulse rate and blood pressure.

Even more marked is the therapeutic value of *Taiji Quan*. This combination of *wushu* and traditional breathing and physical exercise uses the mind to lead movement, keeping the muscles as relaxed as possible, and not using too much force. During practice, external interference should be excluded as completely as possible, allowing the mind to enter a relaxed, controlled state. In this way it will rest and recuperate. At the same time, relaxed, controlled movements allow the blood to circulate freely without restriction from locked joints or tense muscles. Breathing becomes unrestricted and deep, while the gentle exercise gradually stimulates the internal organs and the cardio-vascular system without the practitioner becoming exhausted or out of breath. Thus vitality, concentration and strength develop naturally according to the condition of the practitioner, especially good for the ill, weak or elderly.

A medical research unit in Shanghai made a 17-month comparative study on patients with irregular blood pressure. The results showed that among the group who, in addition to receiving medicinal treatment practised *Taiji Quan* every day, 43 percent experienced a significant drop to healthy levels in blood pressure, and 83 percent achieved a return to normal rates on the electrocardiogram. However, among the group receiving only medicinal treatment, the respective figures were only 8 percent and 20 percent. Shanghai's Tongji University also made a study on 493 regular practitioners of *Taiji Quan* among its teachers and students. It discovered that their vitality, stamina, sleep and digestion had all improved.

2. Self-Defence Skills

Historically, *wushu* was primarily concerned with warfare. It was a training method developed for self-defence. Today, it still maintains distinct combat characteristics and a few styles still stress the practice and development of effective combat skills.

Recent centuries have seen many great *wushu* masters. They made great strides in combining combat skills with healthy training methods designed to train both the mind and body and to give full rein to the body's natural abilities.

3. The Beauty of Chinese *Wushu*

Wushu is not just a way to enhance one's health and skills. Its long association with dance has lent it an enriching artistic quality. At the same time, its emphasis on posture, composure, self-control, spirit and lively exercise imbues it with a beautifying effect on the physique, and a positive effect on the character. These qualities turn *wushu* into *wuyi*—martial artistry.

Historically, *wushu* has been closely related to the arts, especially music and dance. As early as the Zhou Dynasty (11th century B.C.–221 B.C.) dance was used as a stimulant on the eve of battle. By the Tang Dynasty (618-907), the two had become thoroughly intertwined. In *Prince Qin's Dance of Military Victory*, "128 entertainers danced, clad in armour and gripping halberds."

The famous painter Wu Daozi and the calligrapher Zhang Xu, both of the Tang period, were greatly inspired in their work by a sword dance they saw. The

Tang poet Du Fu praised a martial dance:

> *The many spectators are greatly surprised;*
> *Moved are even Heaven and Earth.*
> *The advancing movements are a thunderbolt,*
> *The retreating ones a raging storm;*
> *They stop like sea waters frozen in the clarity of dawn.*

Wushu can also greatly enhance the appearance, giving a well-proportioned, co-ordinated, agile physique, and a composed and lively spirit. In classical times, *wushu* masters were praised as being "calm like an elegant woman, yet a fierce tiger when disturbed."

4. Virtue and Skill

Another characteristic of Chinese *wushu* is its emphasis on self-control and good character. Martial virtue requires that a person exercises self-restraint, never abusing his abilities for personal gratification or to oppress those weaker than himself. He should seek to uphold justice, remain fearless in the face of brutality, and cultivate modesty and a spirit of co-operation.

The monks at the Shaolin Monastery in modern Henan Province laid down the Ten Commandments of *Wushu* practice, among which was the following:

> "Let strengthening the body and mind be the chief aim.... Proficiency in the martial art is only to be used for self-defence. Guard against all indulgence in one's personal vigour. As to any who shows pleasure in provoking disturbances or displaying unwarranted ferocity, the offender shall be dealt with in the same manner as any offending the rules of this establishment."

The spirit of these monks as well as other *wushu* masters of the past and of today are a model to us.

Chapter Three
An Introduction to Some *Wushu* **Styles**

In this chapter, we shall look more closely at three of the most popular schools of Chinese *wushu*: *Chang Quan*, *Taiji Quan* and *Shaolin Quan*. Each is accompanied by an illustrated routine for beginners, with instructions for practice.

I. *Chang Quan*

1. **Evolution and Characteristics**

The name *Chang Quan* was first found in Qi Jiguang's work which mentioned 32 forms of *Chang Quan*. Later, however, the term *Chang Quan* gradually became a name referring to a variety of traditional northern schools of *wushu*, rather than to a distinct individual form. Hence, *Chang Quan* now refers to such styles as *Zha Quan, Hua Quan, Pao Quan, Hong Quan, Hwa Quan, Fanzi Quan, Chuo Jiao* and *Shaolin Quan* and *Tan Tui*. All have strong, swift and extended movements, with many leaps and turns. In combat they emphasize taking initiative in attack, making long strikes, advancing and retreating swiftly and seeking to beat the opponent by speed. In 1920, the *wushu* theorist, Xu Zhedong, described these styles in his work *An Outline of Chinese Wushu*:

> Everything centres around liveliness and speed; attacking and retreating with speed, mobile and unpredictable, keeping the opponent guessing and trying to exploit any opening, with the result that the opponent is too preoccupied to devise effective defence.
>
> It makes use of rapid advance and retreat, moving far, attacking long and taking advantage of distance. Hence its name *Chang Quan* (Extended or Long Boxing).

After the founding of New China, the Physical and Culture and Sports Commission created new forms according to the common characteristics of traditional *Chang Quan* styles. Set teaching materials and competitive regulations were published, promoting the development and popularity of *Chang Quan*, or as the modified form is known, *New Chang Quan*.

New Chang Quan is suitable as a basic practice for developing *wushu* skills, as well as for competition. It is popular among the young people. Many outstanding *Chang Quan* sportsmen and sportswomen have emerged, Li Lianjie being one of the most famous.

New Chang Quan is characterized by fast and vigorous, as well as slower movements. The demands on the joints, muscles and ligaments develop as the intensity of the movements progress. While maintaining the characteristics of traditional *Chang Quan* styles, *New Chang Quan* is more artistic, smoother and more graceful. This has made it easier for practitioners to develop the required skills and agility.

New Chang Quan is based on individual routines,

although basic exercises and dual routines are also practised. The individual routines take two forms:

(A) Set Routines: There are three levels laid down by the Physical Culture and Sports Commission. Each level incorporates bare-hand, broad-sword, rapier, lance and staff forms, each level progressively more difficult, with different movements demanding different techniques and intensity.

(B) Free-Style Routines: The performer selects his own movements, bearing in mind the specifications, level and composition of routines. For national *wushu* competitions, the regulations require at least three main hand-work patterns, five main foot-work patterns, more than five types of fist and palm strikes, three sets of balanced movements and leaps, and four sets of kicking methods, plus flips and tumbles. The whole routine should last not less than one minute and 20 seconds.

Along with *New Chang Quan*, the traditional styles are still preserved and have become popular in recent years. There are no uniform regulations governing the content, composition and level of these routines. This gives full rein to the distinctive styles of the traditional schools, such as the flexible and agile movements of *Zha Quan*; the rapid alternating strikes characteristic of *Fan-zi Quan*; and the emphasis on kicking in *Chuo Jiao* and *Tan Tui*.

2. Essential Skills

The essential elements in the practice of *Chang Quan* are posture, co-ordination, strength, vitality, rhythm and style. Competitors are evaluated on how successfully they meet the required skills and how they combine them in the routine. The requirements are:

(A) Movement Standards

The *Chang Quan* movements and postures are known as the framework. This includes posture, the pose maintained between movements as well as the movements themselves.

Movement standards demand that during practice and competition, posture and the movements are correct. This is an essential point upon which all other skills are developed. Movement standards account for 60 percent of the total score during competitions.

Correct posture means that the upper and lower limbs, as well as the torso, must conform with specified demands for each pose, including midair poses. For instance, the bow stance requires that the front leg is bent at 90° and the back leg is straight, and the riding stance, that the upper-leg is horizontally level. Standard posture requires that the head is upright, neck straight, shoulders level, chest out, back erect and the waist low.

Exact movements refer to the four basic skills of striking, kicking, throwing and manipulation, to immobilize the opponent. Each combat technique; advance or retreat, rise and fall, tumble or roll, leap or balance, must be clear and exact, the hands, feet, body and eyes conforming to the standard. Speed, strength, height, stability and loudness must also conform to requirements. For instance, pushing, stabbing, chopping, slicing and pulling are all attacking methods using the open hand, but each is different. The direction of the strike, the source of force and the point of attack are all different, and they must be precisely distinguished. The *Chang Quan* saying, "Fist like a shooting star, eye movements like lightning; waist like a lithesome snake, feet firm like glue."

(B) Co-ordination

Chang Quan demands perfect co-ordination of the hands, eyes, body and feet, limbs and joints. In addition, concentration, spirit, breathing and strength must be integrated with the movements. Two terms frequently met with in *wushu* are the "three sections" and the "six conformations". The first refers to the division of the body into upper, middle and lower sections which must be completely co-ordinated. The second term refers to the co-ordination of hands and feet, shoulders and hips, elbows and knees, the spirit and mind, the mind and breath, and the breath and strength. This expresses the requirement, essential to *wushu* styles, of complete unity of the body.

(C) Use of Strength

Wushu emphasizes strength. *Chang Quan* demands the full use of strength in combat, quick and precise action and co-ordination of breath and strength. Movements should be crisp, fast, concentrated and snappy. However, one must ensure that one's strength never becomes stiff or inflexible.

(D) Concentration

Both form and spirit must be developed. One's attention must be concentrated, and spirit alert and determined. Eye expression is crucial and must be intimately co-ordinated with movement. Where the hands move, the eyes follow with absolute concentration. However, concentration should not be expressed through tension in the face, frowning, clenched teeth, or wild shouts. Expression should remain calm and composed and movements determined.

(E) Clear Rhythm

Chang Quan is composed of many changes, juxtaposing slow and fast, still and vigourous, rising and falling and tense and relaxed movements. These alternations give the excercise fluctuating and lively rhythm. Without rhythm the form would be stiff and monotonous. "Moving like waves, towering like a mountain, darting like a monkey, descending like a magpie, standing like a rooster, remaining erect like a pine, turning like a wheel, bending like a bow, light like a tree leaf, heavy like a piece of iron, moving as slowly as an eagle, acting as quickly as wind." These comparisons vividly describe the rhythm of *Chang Quan*.

(F) Distinct Style

Each form of *wushu* displays a distinct style through different postures, techniques, strength and rhythms. The movements should be bold, agile, quick and fluid.

3. Illustrated Basic Exercises

1) HAND POSITIONS:

· Fist: Fingers clenched tightly, with the thumb across the forefinger and the second joint of the middle finger (Fig. 1).

Main points: The front plane should be even and the fist tight.

Palm: Five fingers together with thumb bent to the palm and other four fingers stiff (Fig. 2).

Main points: With the change of use of palm, stretch out the thumb to make a V-shaped palm, overlap the other four fingers to make a "ridged-tile" palm.

Form a Hook: keep the first joint of the five fingers

Fig. 1

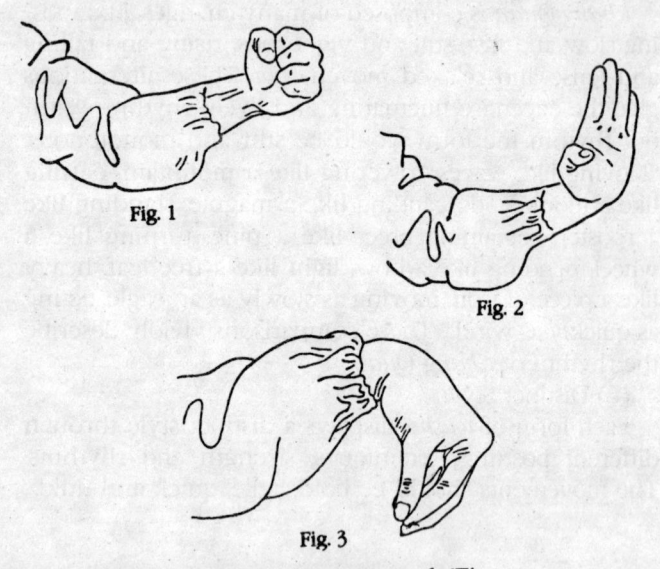

Fig. 2

Fig. 3

together and the wrist bent inward (Fig. 3).

Main point: Do not overbend the fingers.

2) HAND TECHNIQUE
(1) Fist Strike:
a. Feet apart as wide as the shoulders and fists on the hips with the centre of the palms upward (Fig. 4,1).
b. Stretch out the right fist forcefully while turning the forearm and the centre of the palm downward at shoulder level with the force reaching the fist (Fig. 4,2).
c. Stretch out the left fist while turning the centre of the palm downward; take back the right fist to the right side of the rib with the centre of the palm upward (Fig. 4,3).

Practise repeatedly.

Main points: Turn the waist and shoulder when stretching out the fists. Chest out and arms straight. The strike should be fast, forceful. Keep the fists as close to the ribs as possible and the fist should go straight forward.

(2) Palm Strike

a. Preparation posture: Same as that of the Fist Strike.
b. Change the right fist to a palm while turning the forearm inward and stretching it out forward as shoulder level. Keep the fingers pointed upward and turn the palm sidewards (Fig. 5,1).
c. Change the left fist to a palm and strike forward. Clench the right fist and rest it on the right side of the rib (Fig. 5,2).

Practise repeatedly, alternating the right hand with the left.

Main points: Turn the waist and shoulder, thrust the chest forward and straighten the arms, keep the wrists slightly bent and fingers turned upward. The movements should be fast and forceful. When pushing or pulling, the fists should move as close to the ribs as possible.

(3) Arm Brace

a. Preparation posture: Same as that of the Fist Strike (Fig. 6,1).
b. Swing the right hand to the left and then overhead with the fist hole facing slightly downward. Keep the right arm slightly bent and turn the head to the left (Fig. 6,2).
c. Swing the left hand to the right and then overhead while putting down the right fist on the right side of the rib (Fig. 6,3).

Practise repeatedly, alternating the right hand with

the left.

Main points: The arms turned, wrists held downward, head naturally raised, shoulders sloping and elbows slightly bent.

(4) Exposing the Palm

a. Preparation posture: Same as that of the Fist Strike.
b. Open the right fist, swing the arm to the right and overhead, turn the wrist, with the palm upward, turn the head to the left (Fig. 7,1).
c. Open the left fist, swing the arm to the left and overhead, turn the wrist, with the palm upward, turn the head to the right. (Fig. 7,2).

Practise repeatedly, alternating the right hand with the left.

Main points: When turning the palm upward, keep the wrist downward, fingers turned upward, shoulders sloping and elbow slightly bent. Turn the head when turning the wrist and turning the palm upward, which should be done briskly and forcefully.

(5) Forming a Hookhand and Exposing Palm

a. Preparation posture: Same as that of the Fist Strike (Fig. 8,1).
b. Open the right fist and raise it forward from the side of the rib with the palm upward and eyes looking at the palm (Fig. 8,2).
c. Open the left fist, raise it from the side of the rib, and at the same time, swing the right hand to the left and over head, turn the wrist and expose the palm upward; swing the raised left hand to the left and then the back, change the palm to form a hook with the hand, the fingers pointing upward and eyes looking left ahead (Fig. 8,3).
d. Swing the left hand still with a hook from the back

over head, turn the wrist and expose the palm; pull the right hand to the side of the rib and swing it to the right and the back, change the palm to form a hook with the hand, eyes looking ahead (Fig. 8,4-5).

Main points: When moving the two arms, keep the shoulders lowered and the arms straight; turn the waist as the arms move to the left or right; the palm exposing upward and form a hook with the hand turning at the same time the waist and head.

(6) Swinging Palms

a. Preparation posture: Same as that of the Fist Strike.
b. Swing the arms from the left to the right side of the body at shoulder level, with the wrists lowered, fingers pointed upward and eyes following the right hand (Fig. 9,1).
c. Swing the arms to the left side of the body at shoulder level, with wrists lowered, fingers pointed upward and eyes following the left palm (Fig. 9,2).

Main points: When Swinging the palms, turn the head at the same time and keep the shoulders loose and arms straight.

(7) Slicing

a. Preparation posture: Stand with feet parallel to each other and cross the fists in front (Fig. 10,1).
b. Raise the arms and then chop to each side of the body at shoulder level with the thumb-side of the fist facing upward, eyes gazing at the right fist (Fig. 10,2).
c. Put down the fists, cross the arms, raise to shoulder level and chop to each side, eyes gazing at the left fist (Fig. 10,3).

Main points: Keep the shoulders relaxed and arms straight. The chopping motion should be forceful and coordinate with turning the head.

Fig. 4,1   Fig. 4,2   Fig. 4,3

Fig. 5,1   Fig. 5,2   Fig. 6,1

Fig. 6,2   Fig. 6,3   Fig. 7,1   Fig. 7,2

Fig. 8,1

Fig. 8,2

Fig. 8,3

Fig. 8,4

Fig. 8,5

Fig. 9,1

Fig. 9,2

Fig. 10,1

Fig. 10,2

Fig. 10,3

3) STANCES
(1) Bow Stance
Bend the left leg with the toes pointing forward or slightly inward, the knees vertical with the toes; keep the right leg straight with the toes pointing outward; place feet firmly on the ground, heels facing each other; put the hands on the hips, and keep the body straight and eyes level (Fig. 11).

Main points: Keep the front leg bent, back leg straight, chest out and waist low.

(2) Riding Stance

Stand with feet parallel, feet apart, knees bent, upper leg nearly parallel to the ground, hands or palm-up, fists on hips and eyes level (Fig. 12).

Main points: Chest out, waist low, head raised, shoulders sloping and knees pointing slightly inward.

(3) Extending Stance

Keep the left knee bent, both knees slightly pointing outward, the right leg straight, toes pointing inward, hands extended, or fists on hips, eyes looking ahead (Fig. 13).

Repeat on the other side.

Main points: Chest out, waist straight, hips low, body bent slightly forward, feet firmly on the ground.

(4) Light-step Stance

Keep the right leg bent in a half-squatting postion, with foot turned outward about 45 degrees; take a half step foward with the left foot, lift the heel, with the toes lightly touching the ground, knee bent and pointing slightly inward, weight on the back leg; hands on the hips and look ahead (Fig. 14).

Repeat with the other leg.

Main points: Chest out, waist low, keep the front leg light and the weight on the back leg, upper body bent slightly forward.

(5) Stance

Stand with legs apart, upper body turned to the right; put the right foot horizontally in front of the left one, bend the knees in a squatting position, with the right foot firmly on the ground; lift the left heel, toes pointing ahead, buttocks as close to the left heel as possible; hands or palm-up fists on the hips, eyes looking ahead (Fig. 15).

Repeat with the other leg.

Main points: Chest out, waist straight, one leg in front of the other as close as possible.

(6) Cross-Legged Sitting

Stand with legs apart, the upper body turned to the left; put the left leg in front of the right, bend the right leg and sit down with the outer side of the leg and foot on the ground and buttocks on the heel; stretch the left leg, with the whole foot or the outer side of the foot on the ground, keep upper leg close to the chest and upper body turned to the left as far as possible; fists on the hips or crossed in front, eyes looking back over the left shoulder (Fig. 16).

Repeat with the other leg.

Main points: Chest out, waist straight, upper body turned to the left and bent slightly forward.

(7) T-Stance

Bend the right knee in a half-squatting position; bend the left knee, lift the left heel with toe on the ground, weight on the right leg, hands or palm-up fists on hips, eyes ahead (Fig. 17).

Repeat with the other leg.

Main points: Chest out, waist low, and weight on one leg.

(8) Crossing Stance

Stand with legs wide apart, upper body turned to the right, right toes pointing outwards and right knee bent; stretch out the left leg backwards, with toes pointing ahead and heel lifted up; hands on hips or swaying backward, upper body turned backward from right side and eyes looking back (Fig. 18).

Repeat with the other leg.

Main points: Chest out, waist low, body turned, front leg bent and back leg straight.

Fig. 11

Fig. 12

Fig. 13

Fig. 14

Fig. 15

Fig. 16

Fig. 17   Fig. 18

4) FOOTWORK
(1) Attacking Step

a. Preparation posture: Stand with legs apart, the left leg in front; raise the arms horizontally with fingers pointing upward, and body turned slightly to the left (Fig. 19,1).
b. In rapid succession: front leg bent, upper body bent slightly forward, back foot lifted with front foot on the ground and jumping forward; when in midair, touch the heel of the front foot with the instep of the back foot (Fig. 19,2).
c. Land on the ground with back foot first, eyes looking ahead (Fig. 19,3).

Main points: When in midair, keep the upper body and legs straight.

(2) Stamping Step

a. Preparation posture: Same as that of the Attacking Step.
b. Weight moved to the front and right foot lifted (Fig. 20,1).
c. Lift the left foot and put the right foot where the left foot was, land with the left foot in front of the right foot, eyes gazing ahead (Fig. 20,2).

Fig. 19,1

Fig. 19,2

Fig. 19,3

Fig. 20,1

Fig. 20,2

Fig. 21,1

Fig. 21,2

Fig. 22,1

Fig. 22,2

Fig. 22,3

Fig. 22,4

Main points: Bend the knee when lifting the left foot and land with force; keep the upper body straight and turned half-way back.

(3) Jumping Step

a. Jump forward, bend the left knee horizontally, turn the body to the left and raise the hands (Fig. 21,1).
b. Land with the right foot first and the left foot in front (Fig. 21,2).

Main points: Head raised, waist straight, body turned and legs apart.

(4) Arc Step

a. preparation posture: same as that of the Attacking Step.
b. Step forward with right foot, with palms spread at shoulder level, left palm facing front and right palm facing rear (Fig. 22,1).
c. Upper body bent slightly forward, with left leg stepping forward one step, toes turned outward, body turned to the right with eyes looking back over the right shoulder (Fig. 22,2).
d. Put the right foot in front of the left, with toes pointing inward and without turning the upper body (Fig. 22,3).
e. Take a step forward to the left with toes pointing outwards, and swing the foot in an arc. (Fig. 22,4).

Main points: Chest out, waist bent slightly, legs in a half-squatting position. The swing should be steady and in an arc, with the upper body turned slightly inward and waist and head outward.

5) LEG SKILLS

(1) Pressing

(A) Front Pressing

a. Put one leg on a bar with toes pointing to the head; keep the other leg straight with toes pointing ahead, and hands on the knee (Fig. 23,1).

b. Bend the body forward with head as close to the toes as possible (Fig. 23,2).

Repeat with the other leg.

Main points: keep the upper body, knees and supporting leg straight, foot flexed and bend the body steadily downward.

(B) Side Pressing

Stand with the side of the body facing the bar, put one leg on the bar foot flexed; keep the supporting leg straight with the foot parallel to the bar; on the side of the supporting leg raise the hand over the head and put the other hand in front of the chest. Press down the body with the head as close to the toes as possible (Fig. 24).

Repeat on the other side.

Main points: Chest out, hips relaxed, waist and legs straight and toes turned backward.

(C) Back Pressing

Stand with back facing the bar, put one leg on the bar with the sole facing upward; raise the hands above the head, back bent and pressed backward with head as close to the heel as possible. Press steadily harder (Fig. 25).

Repeat with the other leg.

Main points: Chest out, waist low, head raised, hips relaxed, back leg straight and supporting leg slightly bent.

(D) High Position Pressing

Same as the Front, Side and Back pressings. Only the bar should be higher than shoulder level (Fig. 26,1-2).

Main points: To keep balance, hold something for support.

(E) Low Position Pressing (in three postures)

a. Front: Same as Front Pressing. Keep supporting leg bent in a half-squatting position, the other leg stretched forward with heel on the ground and toes turned upward (Fig. 27,1).

b. Side: Same as Side Pressing. Keep the supporting leg bent in a half-squatting position, the other leg stretched out sideways with the heel on the ground and toes turned upward (Fig. 27,2).

c. Side Extension: One leg bent in squatting position, and the other extended out sideways with the hand holding the toes, the upper body pressed down as hard as possible (Fig. 27,3).

Repeat with the other leg.

Main points: For the Side Extension, keep the waist straight, chest out and both feet firmly on the ground.

(2) Pulling

(A) Holding and Pulling

Keep one leg straight as support, the other bent and lifted, with the same-side hand holding the outside of the knee, and the other hand holding the instep; keep upper leg close to the chest, lower leg tightened up and toes turned inward in front (Fig. 28).

Main points: Head raised, waist straight, supporting leg steady and bent leg close to the body.

(B) Front Pulling

a. Do the whole routine for the Holding and Pulling and then straighten the bent leg with toes turned inward (Fig. 29,1).

b. This can also be practised between two persons with one person holding the other's heel in one hand and shoulder in the other. Pull as hard as possible (Fig. 29,2).

Main points: Same as Front Pressing. When doing it

Fig. 23,1

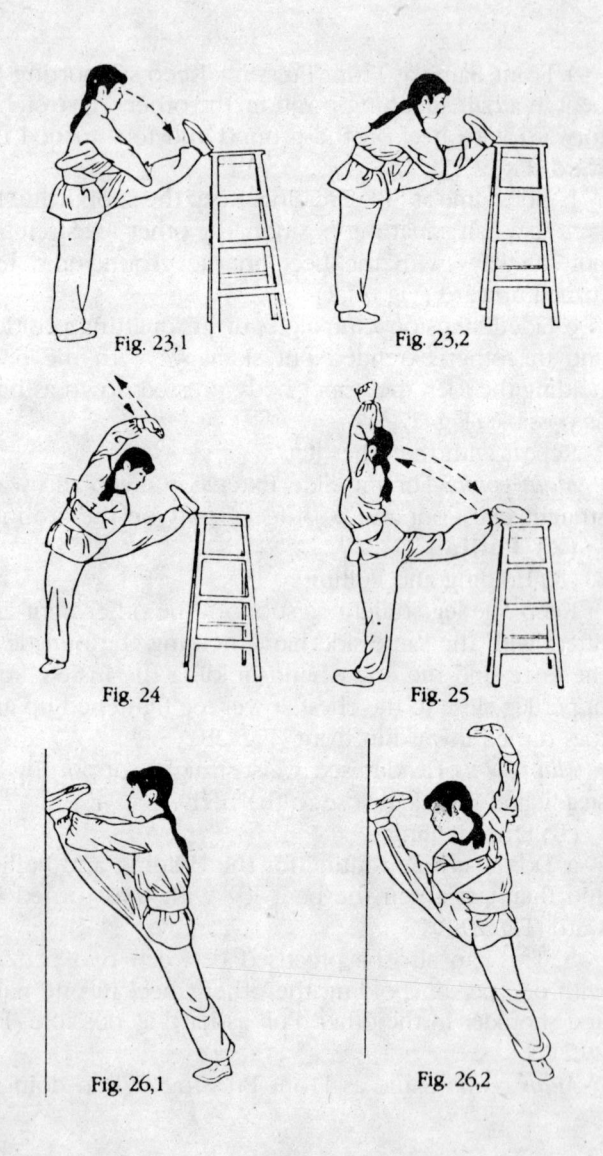

Fig. 23,2

Fig. 24

Fig. 25

Fig. 26,1

Fig. 26,2

Fig. 27,1

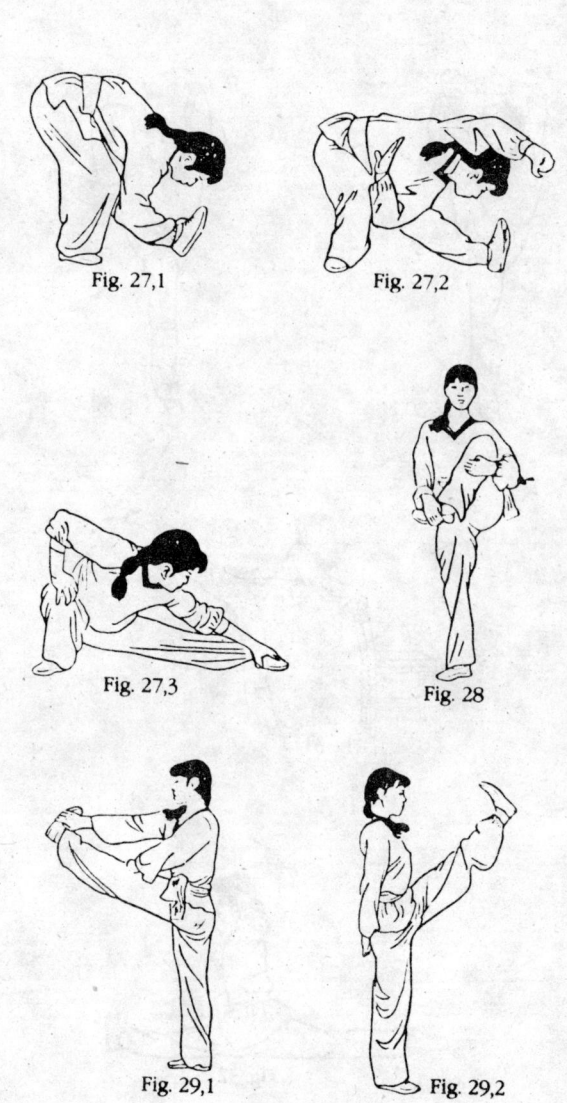

Fig. 27,2

Fig. 27,3

Fig. 28

Fig. 29,1

Fig. 29,2

Fig. 30,1   Fig. 30,2

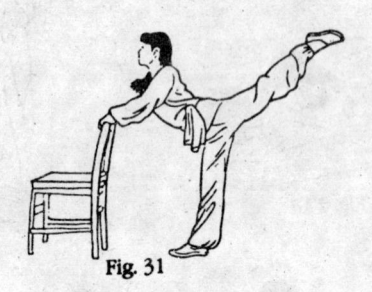

Fig. 31

Fig. 32

between two persons, increase the force of the pull gradually.

(C) Side Pulling

a. Bend and lift a leg with the same-side hand holding the heel from the inner side of the lower leg, hold the leg above the head with the supporting leg straight and steady and the other hand raised over the head (Fig. 30,1).

b. This can also be practised between two persons, with one person holding the other's heel and pushing to the side (Fig. 30,2).

Main points: Same as the Side Pressing. When doing it with the help of another person, the force should be gradual.

(D) Back Pulling

Keep the supporting leg straight with hands holding the bar, and the other leg held up by another person and pulled up and backward (Fig. 31).

Repeat with the other leg.

Main points: Chest out, back bent backward and toes tight.

(3) Split

(A) Forward Split

Place hands on the floor on each side of the body or stretch out the arms to each side and split legs forward with the back side of the front leg on the floor (Fig. 32).

Main points: Chest out, waist straight, and legs straight.

(B) Lateral Split

Stretch out the arms to the front on each side with legs split laterally, the inner side of the leg on the floor (Fig. 33).

Main points: Same as the Forward Split.

(4) Kicking

(A) Front Kick

a. Preparation Posture: Stand with legs close together, raise the arms out to the side at shoulder level with the upper body straight and eyes ahead (Fig. 34,1).

b. Take half a step forward with the right foot, kick with the left foot to forehead level with the toes turned upward and eyes ahead (Fig. 34,2).

c. Put down the left foot with the instep tight, touch the floor lightly with the left toe and take half a step forward, kick with right foot up to the forehead level.

Repeat with the right leg.

Main points: Chest out, hips tight, upper body, waist and leg straight; kick forcefully and put down foot lightly.

(B) Diagonal Kick

Same as the Front Kick. Kick diagonally with toes turned inward (Fig. 35).

Main points: Same as the Front Kick.

(C) Side Kick

a. Preparation Posture: Same as the Front Kick.

b. Take half a step forward with right foot, lift left heel, turn upper body to the right, stretch the left arm forward and right arm backward (Fig. 36,1).

c. Turn the left toes inward and kick to the side to the left ear with right hand raised over the head and the left palm on the right side of the body. (Fig. 36,2)

Repeat with the right leg.

Main points: Chest out, waist straight, hips relaxed, upper body turned to one side but held straight.

(D) Outward Leg Swing

a. Preparation posture: Same as the Front Kick.

b. Take half a step forward with right foot, kick

Fig. 33

Fig. 34,1

Fig. 34,2

Fig. 35

Fig. 36,1

Fig. 36,2

53

Fig. 37,1

Fig. 37,2

Fig. 37,3

Fig. 38,1

Fig. 38,2

Fig. 38,3

diagonally to the right side with left foot, toes turned inward (Fig. 37,1).

c. Swing the left foot from the front to the left side with palm patting the outside of the left foot (Fig. 37,2-3).

d. Bring the left foot down, take half a step forward with the left foot and swing the right foot to the side.

Main points: Chest out, waist low, hips relaxed, and swing the foot as hard as possible to draw a circle.

(E) Inward Leg Swing

a. Preparation posture: Same as the Front Kick.

b. Take half a step forward with the right foot, swing the left foot up in an arc from left to right, toes turned inward (Fig. 38,1).

c. Swing the raised foot in an arc to the right with the sole turned inward and slap the sole of the left shoe with the right hand (Fig. 38,2).

d. Land the left foot on the outside of the right foot (Fig. 38,3), take half a step foward and do the whole routine with the right foot.

Main points: Same as Outward Leg Swing.

(F) Leg Shoot

a. Preparation posture: Hands on hips, legs straight and close together.

b. Take half a step forward with the left foot, raise the right leg with the knee bent so that the knee is slightly higher than the waist, lower the right knee swiftly, straighten the right foot, kick the leg forward above waist level, and keep the upper and lower leg straight (Fig. 39,1-2).

Repeat with the left leg.

Main points: Chest out, waist and knees straight, the kick should be swift and the force of the kick extending to the toes.

(G) Side Kick

a. Preparation posture: Legs crossed in a half-squatting position with hands on hips or crossed in front (Fig. 40,1).

b. Raise the front leg with the knee bent and the toes turned inward, stretch the arms when kicking sideways over the shoulder, with the upper body tilted to one side and eyes looking at the raised foot (Fig. 40,2).

Practise on both sides.

Main points: Knees straight, leg raised high, the force of the kick extended to the heel, the outside of the foot facing upward and supporting leg steady.

(5) Leg Sweep

(A) Front Leg Sweep

a. Preparation posture: Stand with legs wide apart.

b. Keep the right knee bent, upper body and arms turned to the right, and head turned to the left (Fig. 41,1).

c. Keep left knee bent, heel raised, and front sole firmly on the ground; stretch out the right leg, keep it straight with toes turned inward and the sole of the foot on the ground; sweep the ground with the right foot from right to left in an arc, while turning the upper body to the left with left palm turned upward, over the head; hook the right hand behind the back; eyes ahead when turning the body (Fig. 41,2-3).

Main points: Always keep the right leg extended, chest out, back straight, head naturally raised, shoulders lowered and waist turned to the left as much as possible.

(B) Rear Leg Sweep

a. Preparation posture: Keep left knee bent and palms pushing forward (Fig. 42,1).

Fig. 39,1
Fig. 39,2

Fig. 40,1
Fig. 40,2

Fig. 41,1
Fig. 41,2

Fig. 41,3 Fig. 42,1

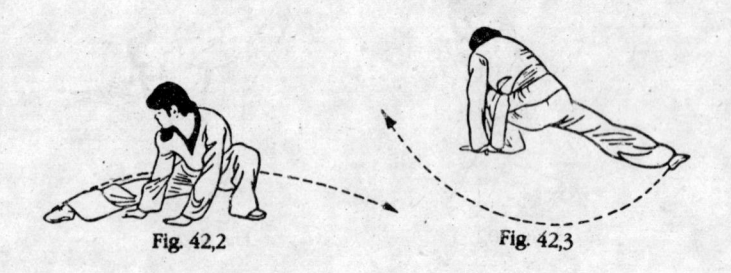

Fig. 42,2 Fig. 42,3

Fig. 42,4 Fig. 43

b. Keep left knee bent in a squatting position, toes turned inward, right leg extended, upper body bent forward and turned to the right, palms placed on the ground close to the right knee (Fig. 42,2).

c. Place two palms on the ground for support, turn the upper body and twist the waist to the right as much as possible, and sweep the ground with the right leg from right to left in an arc in the rear of the body (Fig. 42,3-4).

Main points: Body turned, hands placed on the ground, waist twist should be consistent, and the sweep quick and forceful.

(6) Shoulder Skills

(A) Pressing Shoulders

Stand one step away facing the bar with legs apart, upper body bent, hands holding the bar. Press down as hard as possible (Fig. 43).

Main points: Arms stretched out, legs straight, gradually increase the force, chest out, waistlowered, with the pressing point at the shoulders.

(B) Arm Swing in Full Circle

Stand with legs apart, swing the arms in a circle, clockwise from right to left, and gradually increase the speed of the swing (Fig. 44).

(C) Crossed Swing

Stand with legs apart, arms raised over head; swing the left arm from front to rear in an arc; swing the right arm from rear to front in an arc (Fig. 44,1-3).

Practise with both arms in different directions.

Main points: Shoulders relaxed and upper body turned.

(D) Arm Brandish

a. Preparation posture: Stand with legs wide apart and

arms raised to the side (Fig. 45,1).

b. Upper body turned to the right, left arm raised over head, and swing to the front in an arc, and right arm swung to the rear (Fig. 45,2).

c. Upper body turned to the left with eyes looking ahead, swing the right arm upward and to the right in an arc, swing the left arm downward to the rear (Fig. 45,3).

d. Upper body turned to the left, swing the right arm downward to the front and left in an arc, and swing the left arm upward and to the rear (Fig. 45,4).

e. Upper body turned to the left with eyes looking ahead, swing the right arm upward and to the right and swing the left arm downward and to the left (Fig. 45,5).

f. Upper body turned to the right, swing the right arm downward and to the rear and swing the left arm upward and to the front (Fig. 45,6).

g. Keep on turning the upper body and swinging arms. The two arms should always be in opposite directions.

Main points: Turning the body should give drive to the arm swing; keep shoulders relaxed, arms stretched, body flexible and coordinated with arm swing.

(7) Waist Skills

(A) Bend at the Waist

a. Stand with legs together, hands clasped above the head, palms turned upward (Fig. 46,1).

b. Bend over with palms reaching for the ground (Fig. 46,2).

c. Hold the ankles with both hands and bend the head and chest to the legs (Fig. 46,3).

Main points: Legs straight without bending the knees; chest out, waist low and hips tight.

Fig. 44,1

Fig. 44,2

Fig. 44,3

Fig. 45,1

Fig. 45,2

Fig. 45,3

Fig. 45,4

Fig. 45,5

Fig. 45,6

Fig. 46,1

Fig. 46,2

Fig. 46,3

(D) Waist Swing

Stand with legs apart and swing the upper body and the arms together from the left, rear, right, to the front. At the same time, swing the waist in the same direction of arm swing (Fig. 47).

When practising, swing in turn in opposite directions.

Main points: Arm swing should give drive to the body swing and be consistent; gradually add force and speed to the swing.

(C) Waist Twist

a. Upper body bent forward with the left leg back behind the right leg, arms swung to the right (Fig. 48,1).

b. Using the front soles of the feet as axles, twist the waist, turn the upper body to the left, bend back the chest and swing the arms forcefully to the left (Fig. 48,2).

c. Turn the body to the left and swing the arms to the left with the chest and stomach in (Fig. 48,3).

d. Twist the waist to the right and turn the upper body to the right using the front soles of the feet as axles.

Main points: When twisting the waist, press down the foot with chest and stomach out, the movement should be fast and forceful.

(8) Jumping

(A) Kicking in the Air

a. Preparation Posture: Stand with the left foot slightly touching the ground, and raise two arms with palms facing front and rear (Fig. 49,1).

b. Take half a step forward with the left foot, then a step forward with the right foot with knees bent (Fig. 49,2).

c. Jump with the left knee bent or straight, swing the left leg upward and kick in midair; swing the arms to the front and over head and clap the back of the right hand quickly with the left palm (Fig. 49,3).

d. When in midair, swing the right leg forward and kick with the instep stretched tight, right hand swiftly tapping the right instep, take back the left knee and bend in front of the chest with toes pointing downwards; swing the left hand to the left with the upper body bent slightly forward, eyes ahead (Fig. 49,4).

Main points: Keep chest out, waist straight, the swing of the right foot should be higher than waist level.

(B) Whirlwind Kicking

a. Preparation posture: Same as that of Kicking in the Air.

b. Take a step forward with the right foot, toes turned inward and the body turned to the left and bent forward for jumping (Fig. 50,1).

c. Swing the arms to the left over head, jump and turn the upper body to the left in a circle, while lifting the left leg and swinging to the left; raise the right leg turned slightly to the left and tap the instep of the right foot with the left hand in front (Fig. 50,2).

d. Finish turning the upper body a complete circle and land on the left foot followed by the right foot.

Main points: All the movements should coordinate with each other. When jumping in the air, keep the head naturally raised, waist straight, leg-swing should be forceful and unrestricted, and tap the foot in front.

(C) Swing in the Air

a. Jump with the right foot, raise the arms with the right palm facing front and the left palm facing rear, bend the upper body slightly and turn it outward (Fig. 51,1).

b. Land with the right foot, then the left, take a step

forward with the right foot in an arc, toes turned outward, body weight low and upper body bent slightly backwards (Fig. 51,2-3).

c. Jump with the right foot, kick to the right side with the left leg, and swing the arms over head (Fig. 51,4).

d. When in midair, turn the body to the right with the right leg swung outward; tap the instep of the right foot with the left hand first, right hand second; bend the left leg to the chest or keep it straight, and swing to the left with the upper body slightly bent forward (Fig. 51,5).

Main points: The step forward should be an arc, the jump with the right foot forceful, toes turned outward, and coordinated with all movements, such as the waist twist and the turn of the body; when swinging outward with the right leg, the swing should be forceful and unrestricted, and the left leg slightly bent or straight by the side, tap the foot in front.

(D) Spinning

a. Preparation posture: Stand with legs apart.

b. Swing the waist and arms to the right, with upper body turned to the right and bent slightly forward (Fig. 52,1).

c. Move the body weight to the left, bend the upper body forward and spin leftward and to the rear (Fig. 52,2).

d. Jump with left foot, stretch out the arms to the rear and spin the right leg to the rear and to the right (Fig. 52,3-4).

e. Spin in midair, body parallel to the ground (Fig. 52,5).

F. Land with the right foot first and keep spinning the body with the sole of the right foot as the axle (Fig. 52,6).

Main points: Spin one circle in the air with the waist bent, chest out, waist low and legs swung in turn to the right and to the rear.

(9) Balancing

(A) Knee-Raised Balancing

Stand with hands on hips, one leg straight and the other lifted and bent in front, pointing the toes down and inward (Fig. 53).

Main points: Keep the supporting leg steady and straight, head raised, upper body and waist straight, shoulders sloping, and the lifted leg bent as much as possible.

(B) Swallow Balancing

Stand with one leg as the support and another lifted, hands crossed in front. Bend the upper body forward, stretch the other leg to the rear with the arms raised to each side (Fig. 54).

Main points: Keep the supporting leg steady and straight, stretch the leg to the rear as high as possible with toes pointed, knee straight, chest out, waist lowered and head raised.

(C) Looking-at-the-Moon Balancing

Stand with one foot as the support, stretch the other to the rear, the knee bent and toes pointed; bend the upper body forward and twist the body to the side of the supporting leg, arms raised to each side of the body, eyes looking to the rear (Fig. 55).

Main points: Keep the supporting leg steady, waist twisted, body turned, head raised, chest out, and the upper leg of the raised leg high.

(10) Combined Exercise for Five Kinds of Steps

(A) Preparation posture: Stand with feet close to one

Fig. 47

Fig. 48,1

Fig. 48,2

Fig. 48,3

Fig. 49,1

Fig. 49,2

Fig. 49,3

Fig. 49,4

Fig. 50,1

Fig. 50,2

Fig. 51,1

Fig. 51,2

Fig. 51,3

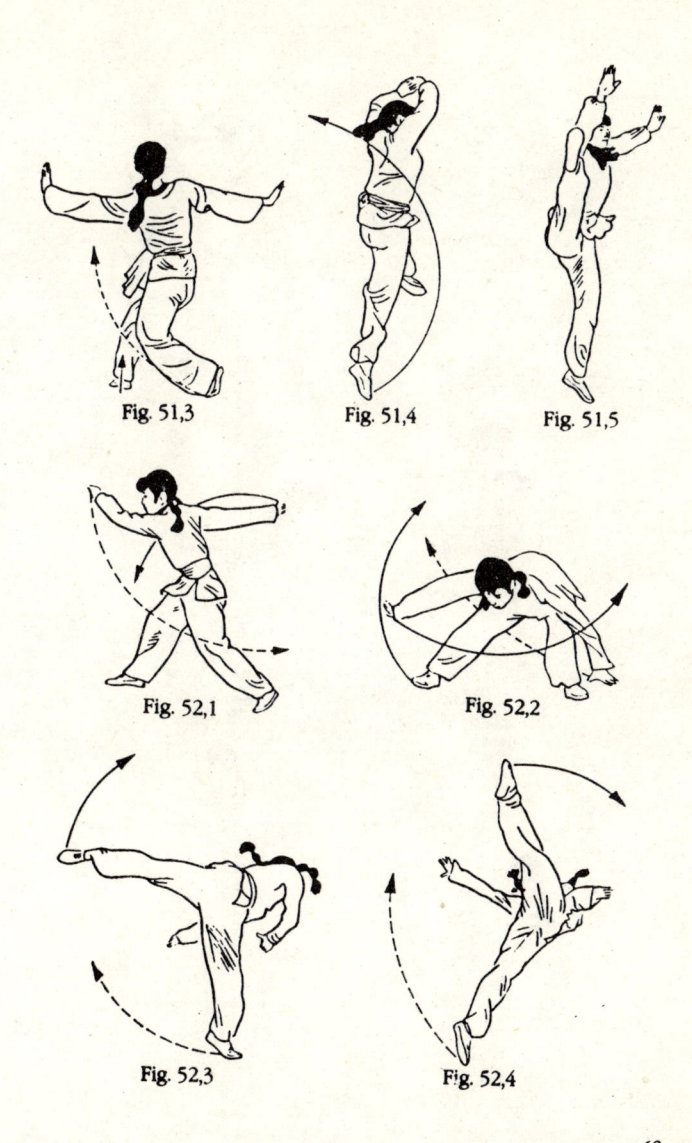

Fig. 51,4

Fig. 51,5

Fig. 52,1

Fig. 52,2

Fig. 52,3

Fig. 52,4

69

Fig. 52,5

Fig. 52,6

Fig. 53

Fig. 54

Fig. 55

Fig. 56

another, fists on hips and palms upward (Fig. 56).

(B) Punching in Bow Stance

Step to the left with the knee bent in a bow stance and make a level sweeping movement with the left hand and return to the hip, and then punch forward with the right fist, eyes ahead (Fig. 57).

(C) Kicking and Punching

Move the body weight forward by kicking forward with the right foot while punching forward with the left fist from the hip with the fist hole facing downward, right fist on the hip and eyes looking ahead (Fig. 58).

(D) Punching with Riding Stance

Turn the upper body to the left, knees bent, legs apart in a half squatting posture; raise the left palm over the head, elbow slightly bent; punch with the right fist to the right side, head turned to the right, eyes following the right fist (Fig. 59).

(E) Palm Striking in Resting Stance

Put the left foot behind the right one while turning the upper body to the left; change the right fist into a palm and strike from over the head down to the left side; change the left palm into a fist and place it on the hip (Fig. 60,1). Bend the knee in a resting stance, punch forward with the left fist change the right palm into fist and place on the hip with eyes following the left fist (Fig. 60,2).

(F) Lifting Knee and Stabbing

Turn the upper body to the left; change the right fist into a palm, stab to the left diagonally by passing the back of the left hand with the palm facing upward, at the same time, change the left fist into palm, take it back to the armpit with the palm facing downward, bend the left knee and raise the left leg with eyes following the right palm (Fig. 61).

(G) Stabbing with Extended Stance

Bend the right knee in a squatting posture and extend the left leg; stab with the left hand from the inner side of the left leg with two arms in a line and eyes following the left palm (Fig. 62).

(H) Lifting Palm with Empty Stance

Bend the left leg in a bow stance, place the right foot forward, toes touching the ground, heel lifted; raise the

Fig. 57

Fig. 58

Fig. 59

Fig. 60,1

Fig. 60,2

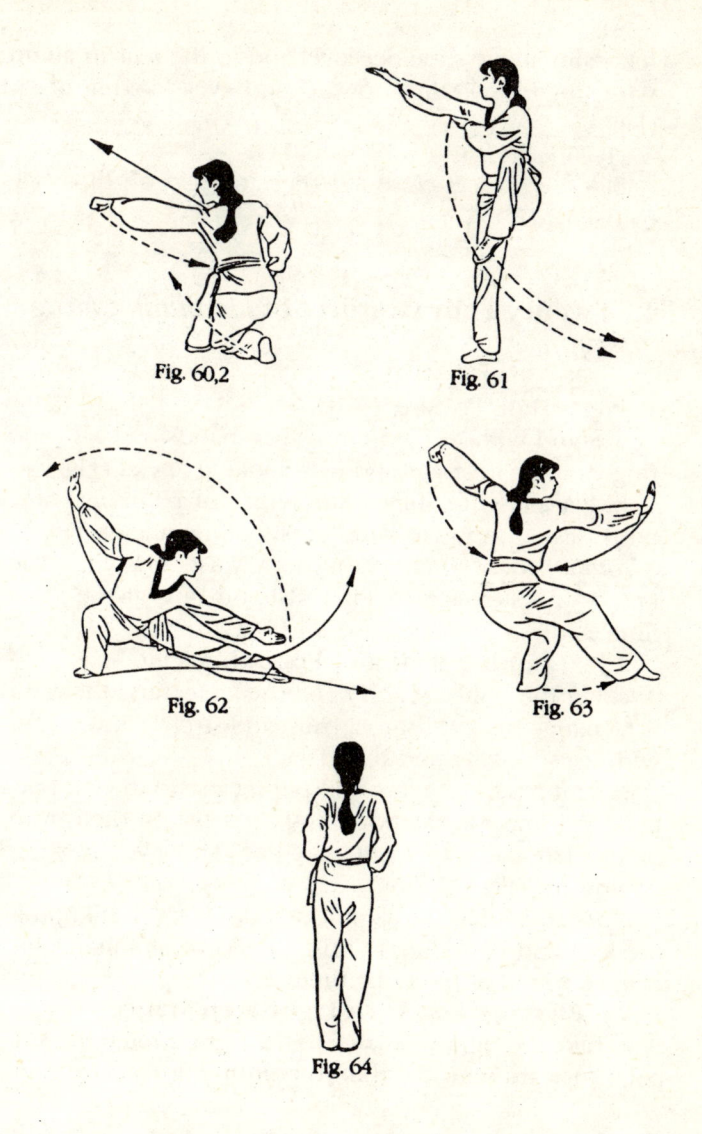

Fig. 61

Fig. 62

Fig. 63

Fig. 64

left palm above shoulder level and to the rear in an arc with fingers pointing upward and eyes looking ahead (Fig. 63).

(I) Finish Posture

Stand with feet close together and fists on hips (Fig. 64).

4. Twenty-Four Gestures of *Lianhuan Chang Quan*

Preparation Posture:

a. Stand with feet close together, hands on each side, fingers close together and eyes looking ahead (Fig. 1).

b. Place fists on hips with centre of palms upward, head turned to the left and eyes looking ahead (Fig. 2).

Main points: Keep chest out, waist straight, head raised, and stomach in. Place fists on hips at the same time as the head turns.

1) Stamping Foot and Pounding Fist

a. Lift the right leg and bend the knee; raise the right fist, change the left fist to a palm and stretch downward with eyes looking ahead (Fig. 3).

b. Stamp the right foot and put it close to the left one; bend the knees while pounding right fist on the centre of the left palm in front of chest with eyes looking downward (Fig. 4).

Main points: Lift the right foot to knee level. Stamping the foot and pounding the fist should be simultaneous. Make a sound at the same time.

2) Piercing Fist with Light-Step Stance

a. Take the right foot back to the right, stretch the left palm forward with the thumb pointing downward and the centre of the palm outward and pull; take the right fist back to the right hip with the palm side upward (Fig. 5).

b. Shift the body weight back to the right leg and take back the left foot with toe touching the ground; keep legs straight with front leg light and back leg steady to form a left light-step stance. At the same time, turn the upper body to the left, swing the left palm to the left in an arc to the hip with a fist; thrust the right fist to the right and forward in an arc and stop in front of the right shoulder with the thumb side facing diagonally downward; turn the head to the left with eyes looking ahead to the left (Fig. 6).

Main points: Keep chest out, stomach in, head raised, knees straight and left toes pointed inward. Turn the head and waist at the same time as thrusting the fist.

3) Punching with Bow Stance

a. Take a step forward and left with the knees bent in a half riding stance; bend the left elbow with the fist a bit higher than shoulder level and the knuckles facing upward; place the right fist on hip with palm upward and eyes following the left fist (Fig. 7).

b. Bend the upper body slightly forward with the left knee bent and the right leg straight in a bow stance; punch the right fist from the hip with palm side downward at the shoulder level; take back the left fist to the hip with the palm upward and eyes following the right fist (Fig. 8).

Main points: When punching, turn the waist and shoulder with force reaching the fist. When in the bow stance, keep back leg as straight as possible without lifting the heel from the ground; keep the front leg bent forward with the knee and toes on the same line.

4) Kicking and Punching

Lift the right leg with the knee bent toes and pointed, kick forward forcefully to shoulder level; punch the left fist forward, eyes looking ahead (Fig. 9).

Main points: Kick the leg forcefully, the knee straight and the supporting leg slightly bent.

5) Punching with a Riding Stance

Move the right foot forward with toes turned inward, the upper body turned to the left and the knees bent in a riding stance, and at the same time, punch the right fist to the right with the fist hole upward; take back the left fist to the hip with the palm side upward eyes following the right fist (Fig. 10).

Main points: When in the riding stance, put the body weight evenly on the two legs with one foot parallel to the other, heels stamping outward, knees turned inward, chest out, waist low and head raised.

6) Sweeping Foot and Striking

a. Step backward with the left foot to the right side of the right foot while swinging the right palm to the front, and then taking it back to the hip side; change the left fist into a palm, stretch out the left palm under the right arm while turning the palm over with the palm centre upward and pull (Fig. 11).

b. Sweep backward with the right foot to form a left bown stance while striking the right palm forward with the palm facing to the left; take back the left fist to the hip, eyes following the right palm (Fig. 12).

Main points: When sweeping the foot and pulling the hand, keep the idea of attacking and defending in mind, sweep with the weight on the heel, strike with the strength going to the base of the palm. The waist and legs should also carry the impulse of the movement.

7) Turning Body and Kicking

a. Turn the upper body to the right on the left heel and right sole, raise the right arm and swing from front to rear, change the left fist to a palm and raise it over the head (Fig. 13).

b. Continue swinging the arms. Raise the right palm over the head with the palm facing upward; extend the left hand to the back to form a hook with the wrist bent upward and fingers close together; kick with the left foot forcefully toward the forehead with foot flexed (Fig. 14).

Main points: Swing arms in full circles with shoulders relaxed. The kick should be swift and forceful, stomach in, head lowered and waist bent.

8) Leaping Forward

a. Step forward with the left foot, bend the knees with the upper body bent forward; swing the right hand to the left and stretch the left hand backward with both palms facing inward, eyes following the left hand (Fig. 15).

b. Lift the right leg with the knee bent, leap forward with the left leg straight while raising the arms in arcs with the head raised, chest out and the eyes following the right palm (Fig. 16).

c. Land with the right foot first with the knee bent in a squatting posture; stretch out the left leg to the left; change the right palm to a fist and place it on the hip, swing the left arm in an arc from over the head downward to the left, and then to the right side of the chest with fingers pointing upward and the eyes looking to the left (Fig. 17).

Main points: The leap should be far and high, the landing light, and stretch the legs fast.

Fig. 1 Fig. 2 Fig. 3

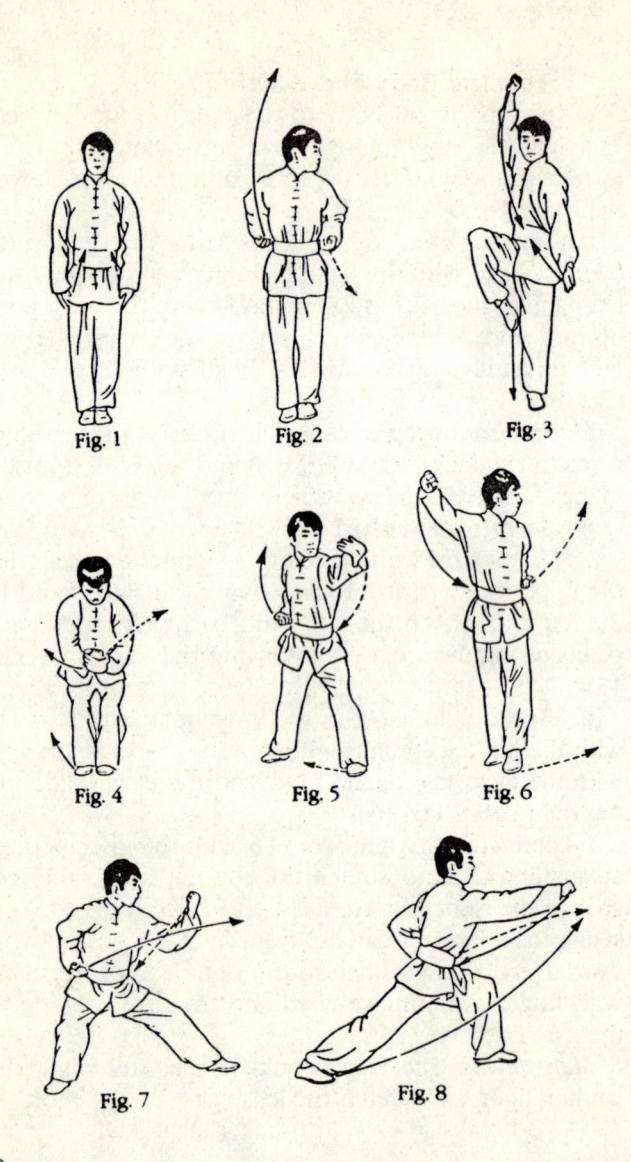

Fig. 4 Fig. 5 Fig. 6

Fig. 7 Fig. 8

Fig. 9

Fig. 10

Fig. 10

Fig. 11

Fig. 12

Fig. 13

Fig. 14

Fig. 15

Fig. 16

Fig. 17

Fig. 18

9) Punching with Bow Stance

Bend the left knee and stretch back the right leg; swing the left arm horizontally in an arc to the hip; punch with the right fist forward from the hip with the palm side downward and the eyes following the right fist (Fig. 18).

Main points: Punch swiftly and forcefully, and move the waist and leg at the same time.

10) Tap the Foot and Punch

a. Stand with the left leg as the support, stretch the right foot and kick forward to shoulder level; change the left fist to a palm and tap the instep of the right foot; take back the right fist to the hip (Fig. 19).

b. After tapping the foot, land on the right foot to make a left bow stance; change the left palm to a fist and place it on the hip, punch the right fist forward (Fig. 20).

Main points: Tap the foot accurately and quickly with the supporting leg slightly bent.

11) Side kick with Twining Hands

a. Put the right foot in front of the left with the toe and the upper body turned to the right, legs crossed, knees bent in a sitting posture and the left palm on the right wrist; turn the right forearm outward, change the right fist to a palm, chop down to make a fist, take back the hands on the right hip side (Fig. 21).

b. Bend the upper body to the right, lift the left leg and bend the knee with the foot flexed and turned inward and kick forcefully to the left over the shoulder eyes following the left foot (Fig. 22).

Main points: Step, turn and place the palm on the wrist at the same time. When kicking, keep the supporting leg slightly bent, the upper body turned to one side, kick with force reaching the sole of the foot.

12) Slicing in Bow Stance

a. Lift the left foot and put it in front of the right foot with the body weight forward; turn the left palm outward and swing forward in an arc (Fig. 23).

b. Take a step forward to make a right bow stance while swinging the right palm from the rear to the front to the head level with the palm diagonally upward; turn the left palm outward and stretch out to hold the front right arm, with eyes looking at the right palm (Fig. 24).

Main points: Swing arms in a diagonal circle. The waist should give force to the shoulder and the shoulder to the arms and palms.

13) Swinging and Punching in Resting Stance

a. Take the left foot forward with toes turned inward; turn the body swiftly to the right with the front soles of the feet as axles and at the same time, swing the fists to the front and rear (Fig. 25).

b. Keep turning the upper body to the right with legs crossed and knees bent to form a resting stance; while turning the body, swinging the arms in full circle, thrust the left fist to the lower front over the right foot with the palm upward; raise the right arm to the rear over the head with the palm diagonally upward, eyes following the left fist (Fig. 26).

Main points: When in resting stance, put one foot parallel in front of the other foot on the ground; keep the rear foot pointed forward and the heel lifted, knees bent with the back knee supporting the outside of the front knee.

14) Penetrating Palm with Extended Step

a. Take a step forward with the left foot, turn the upper body to the right, change the fists to palms and swing arms to each side (**Fig.** 27).

b. Take the right foot back to the rear of the left foot, raise the left palm and swing to the front in an arc and put the right palm to the hip (Fig. 28).

c. Bend the right knee in a squatting posture, extend the left foot to the left, while turning the upper body to the left and stretching the left palm along the inner side of the left thigh forward to the left; stretch the right palm forward to the right, keep arms straight, palms facing forward and eyes following the left palm (Fig. 29).

Main points: When extending the leg, keep one leg bent and the extended leg straight with the soles of the feet firmly on the ground. The arms should be stretched forward and backward diagonally, and the upper body bent to the left.

15) Hitting Foot in Midair

a. Move the body weight to the front and bend the left knee. Lift the feet, jump with the right foot hitting the left, land, and extend the arms to the front and rear with palms facing sideways (Fig. 30-31).

b. Take the right foot one step forward and jump with the left knee bent; at the same time, swing the right arm downward from the rear to the front and clap the back of the right hand with the left palm over the head (Fig. 32-33).

c. When in midair, swing the right foot swiftly upward with the toes pointing down, tap the right instep with the right palm, bend the left knee close to the upper body with toes pointing downward; swing the left arm to the rear slightly higher than shoulder level, and bend the upper body slightly forward with eyes ahead (Fig. 34).

Fig. 19

Fig. 20

Fig. 21

Fig. 22

Fig. 23

Fig. 24

84

Fig. 25

Fig. 26

Fig. 27

Fig. 28

Fig. 29

Fig. 30

Fig. 31

Fig. 32

Fig. 33

Fig. 34

Fig. 35

Fig. 36

Main points: When hitting the foot, keep the upper body bent slightly forward and turned slightly sideways. Tap the instep of right foot when swinging the foot to the highest position, that is, above the waist. Keep the left leg bent, chest out, waist straight and bent slightly forward.

16) Bending Elbow with Bow Stance

a. Bend the right knee and turn the upper body to the left; cover the right fist with the left palm in front of the chest with eyes looking back to the left (Fig. 35).

b. Put the right foot down in front of the left and bend the knee to make a bow stance; bend the right elbow with the elbow pointing forward; push the right fist with the left palm, eyes ahead (Fig. 36).

Main points: Keep the head raised, waist low, shoulders sloping, backside in and upper body straight.

17) Parrying with Light-Step Stance

a. Take the right foot half a step backward to make a right light step, toes touching the ground, heel lifted, knee slightly bent, parry with the fists to the left side of the forehead, turn the left forearm outward with the fist facing outward; turn the right forearm outward with palm facing inward; turn the upper body to the left, eyes looking to the left (Fig. 37).

b. Turn the upper body to the right, parry with the fists to the right side of the forehead, turn the right forearm inward with the palm facing outward; turn the left forearm outward with the palm facing inward and eyes looking to the right (Fig. 38).

Main points: Parry with the fists close to the forehead at the same time as the upper body turns.

18) Striking with Bow Stance

Take the right foot half a step forward and bend the

knee to make a bow stance; change the right fist to a palm, strike forward from the side of the hip with fingers pointed forward, and put the left fist on the hip with palm facing upward and eyes following the right palm (Fig. 39).

Main points: Coordinate turning the upper body with the step forward, and the strike forward with the palm.

19) Swinging Fists with Withdrawn Step

a. Lift the right leg and bend the knee, turning the upper body to the right while hitting the right upper leg with the right fist (Fig. 40).

b. Take the right foot back to the right and put it down to make a right bow stance; swing the right fist in an even arc to the right and stop in front of the right shoulder; change the left fist to a palm and swing it in an even arc to the left, and then to the front before it meets the right wrist; turn the head to the left with eyes looking forward and to the left (Fig. 41).

Main points: When swinging the fists, turn the head with the neck straight, shoulders sloping and the waist low; keep the upper body straight and the backside in.

20) Lifting Leg with Wrists Bent

Bend the left knee and lift it to the chest, move the left arm to the back with the wrist bent and fingers together; raise the right palm over the head and at the same time turn the upper body to the left bend slightly to the left with eyes looking downward and to the left (Fig. 42).

Main points: The leg and arm movements should be forceful, swift and coordinated with one another. When turning the waist, stretch the arms to the front and rear.

21) Raising Fist with Crossed Legs

a. Take the right foot forward, toes turned to the left

(fig. 43).

b. Take the right foot forward, the left foot backward to the right side; swing the left fist in an arc upward to the right and downward to the right; swing the right fist in an arc to the right, downward, along the waist and to the inner side of the left arm before stretching to the front at head level, with the fist slanting upward, eyes following the right fist (Fig. 44).

Main points: Press down the fists before raising them with the arms half-bent. When crossing the legs, keep the front leg bent with the sole of the foot on the ground, and the back leg extended with the front foot on the ground, the body weight on the front leg, and the upper body turned back to the side of the front leg.

22) Turning Waist and Extending Arms

a. Change the fists to palms and extend the arms to each side and swing; bend the upper body slightly forward, use the front soles of the feet as axles and turn the waist back and to the left (Fig. 45-46).

b. After turnig the waist for one cycle, straighten the upper body, bend the knees, put the right heel on the inner side of the left arch with the toes of the right foot on the ground, and raise the heel of the right foot and point on the diagonal; chop downward to the left with the right palm, put the left palm on the inner side of the right forearm with eyes following the right hand (Fig. 47).

c. Take the right foot forward to the right to make right bow stance; turn the upper body to the right, extend the arms to the front and rear with the right palm facing upward and the left palm facing backward, eyes following the right palm (Fig. 48).

Main points: When turning the waist, keep the waist

Fig. 37

Fig. 38

Fig. 39

Fig. 40

Fig. 41

Fig. 41

Fig. 42

Fig. 43

Fig. 44

Fig. 45

Fig. 46

Fig. 47

Fig. 48

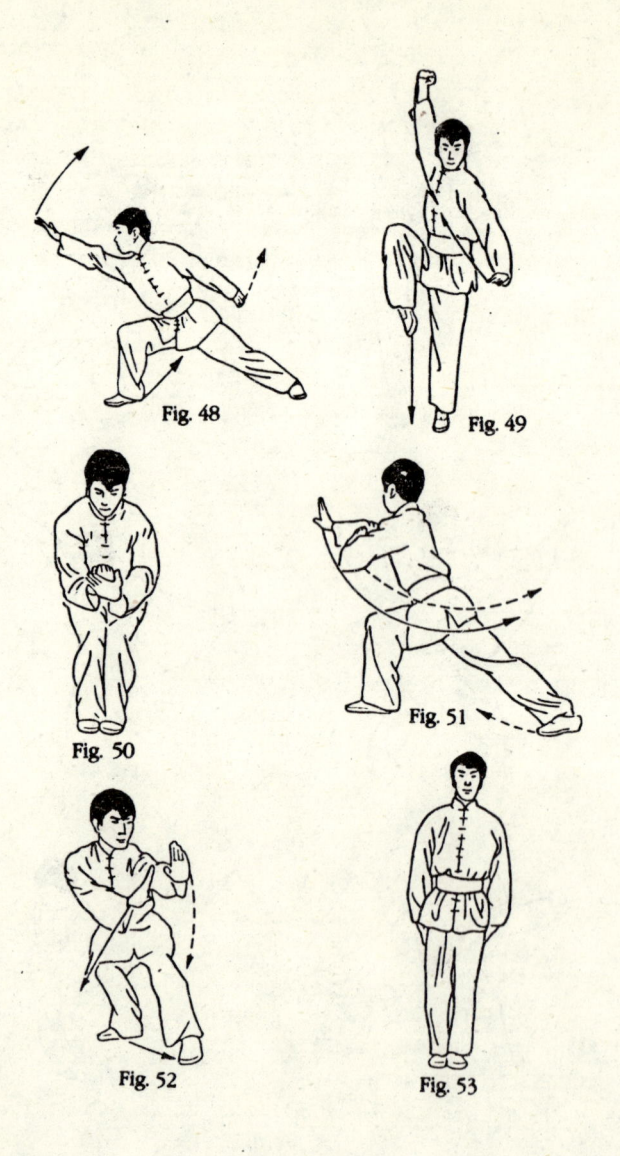

Fig. 49

Fig. 50

Fig. 51

Fig. 52

Fig. 53

and chest straight, bend back the upper body, turn the waist swiftly, and swing the arms lightly but forcefully. Extend the arms at the same time as turning the waist and bending the legs.

23) Stamping Foot and Pounding Fist

Lift the right foot to the inside of the left leg and then stamp the foot; raise the right fist and pound downward on the left palm, with eyes looking downward (Fig. 49-50).

Main points: See 1. Stamping Foot and Pounding Fist.

24) Lifting Palms with Light-Step Stance

a. Take the right foot back to the right side while swinging the palms to the front, upward and to the right; turn the upper body to the right with the head following the right palm (Fig. 51).

b. Move the body weight back to the right leg, bend the left knee slightly with the front sole lightly on the ground, the heel off the ground, and at the same time, turn the upper body to the left, swing the palms in an arc downward and then to the front, higher than shoulder level with the fingers pointing upward and eyes following the left palm (Fig. 52).

Main points: When doing the light step with the knee slightly bent, bend the right knee in a half squatting posture, keep the chest out, waist low and upper body bent slightly forward.

25) Finishing Posture

Move the left foot forward, and the right foot close to the left foot with the arms hanging naturally on each side of the body and eyes looking ahead (Fig. 53).

Main point: See the Preparation Posture.

II. *Taiji Quan*

1. Origin of *Taiji Quan*

As to the origins of *Taiji Quan*, many myths have been passed down from previous centuries. One tradition has it that *Taiji Quan* was developed in the 12th century. At the time of the Song Emperor Huizong (reigned 1101-1126), a Taoist priest at Mount Wudang named Zhang Sanfeng received an imperial summons to the capital, Kaifeng. On the way he was set upon by a band of more than 100 robbers and forced to take refuge. During the night, he was visited in a dream by the Spirit of Mount Wudang, who told him the methods of a *wushu* style. The next day, Zhang used his new skills to drive off the robbers. This style was then passed on through the centuries, becoming known as the "Internal School of Boxing," that is today's *Taiji Quan*.

Another story has it that *Taiji Quan* was developed in the 14th century. This attributes the same Zhang Sanfeng as living between the late Yuan and the early Ming dynasties. He was studying to be a Taoist priest at Mt. Wudang, delving into the mysteries of *yin* and *yang*,* the theory of the "eight trigrams"** and trying to learn the secrets of immortality by observing cranes and tortoises,

---

* According to Chinese philosophy, these are two opposing yet complementary principles in nature, the former feminine and negative, the latter masculine and positive.

** The "eight trigrams" are eight combinations of three whole and broken lines formerly used in divination.

two long-living creatures. One day, he saw a snake and a crane fighting, and eventually developed the 13 *Taiji* postures which form the basis of *Taiji Quan* today.

Such stories are very appealing, but whether or not *Taiji Quan* was developed by Zhang Sanfeng is questionable. Situated in the remote northwest of Hubei Province, Mt. Wudang is noted for its scenic beauty and has been a centre of Taoism since the 7th century. According to historical records preserved at the mountain, there have been two people named Zhang Sanfeng. One, renowned for his combat skills, lived in the Song Dynasty (960-1279); the other, a celebrated Taoist of the early Ming Dynasty (1368-1644), was very adept with a sword. The latter was repeatedly summoned by the reigning emperor, but refused to go, remaining in seclusion. There have been many other tales about this man handed down by the people. Both men combine Taoist spiritual cultivation with their *wushu* skills. Nevertheless, many researchers of *wushu* think there is insufficient evidence to name either one of them as the founder of *Taiji Quan*.

Whatever its earliest origins, *Taiji Quan* can be traced to Wenxian County, Henan Province, for the beginnings of its present form. However, the local people also have two explanations regarding its origins: one, that modern *Taiji Quan* was created at Chenjiagou Village by Chen Wangting; the other, that it was learned in Shanxi Province by Jiang Fa, who then brought it back to his home, Xiaoliu Village, also in Wenxian County.

Both Chen and Jiang were accomplished *wushu* masters of the Ming Dynasty. In 1641, Chen was put in charge of the garrison of his locality and often led his troops into battle. In his later years, he lived in seclusion researching *wushu* methods for self-defence, finally developing a new style of his own. Born in 1574, Jiang Fa became especially skilled in *wushu*. Legend has it that he could catch up with a running hare in 100 paces. Whichever of these men first created or developed it, *Taiji Quan* was gradually transmitted to the outside world. It has three main principles.

1) Assimilation of the essentials and experience of traditional forms of *wushu*. Traditional works on *Taiji Quan* contain many postures and verses, intended as guides to practice, similar to those found in General Qi Jiguang's *Manual of Boxing*, part of his work *A New Work on the Effect of Martial Art* already mentioned. Qi's *wushu* style was a synthesis of sixteen popular schools. *Taiji Quan* is also the cumulation of the development and experience of many popular styles of the time.

2) Assimilation of the traditional methods for cultivating health. *Taiji Quan* appears to have been one of the latest developments in a gradual process which had been going on for centuries, combining *wushu* with traditional forms of internal exercise, meditation and calisthenic exercises for building health and attaining long life. These involved relaxation, concentration and breathing exercises, incorporating a wide variety of methods. Many of these elements can be seen in *Taiji Quan*.

A connection with the Taoist tradition of such methods is mentioned in a poem by Chen Wangting, in which he wrote, "The *Huang Ting* is my constant companion." *Huang Ting* refers to *Huang Ting Jing*, an important early Taoist canon on health through breathing exercises.

3) Assimilation of classical philosophical and medical

theories. *Taiji Quan*, like many of the health exercises mentioned above, adopted the traditional medical theory of promoting the circulation of *qi*, or vital energy in the body to ensure the smooth functioning of the internal organs. It also adopted the philosophical theories of *Taiji*, *yin* and *yang*, *wuxing*,* *bagua*, and others. *Taiji Quan* was originally called the 13 Postures, since it consisted of eight main skills and five main variations. These were associated with the alternations of *bagua* and *wuxing*.

Wang Zongyue, a famous *wushu* practitioner of the 18th century, explained these theories and their application in his *Essays on Taiji Quan*. Assimilating the experiences of previous practitioners, this work was of great value to developing *wushu* and fixing its basic principles. It was from this time that the title *Taiji Quan* was established. *Taiji* refers to the primal state of the universe, the beginning of change. As used here, the term expresses the idea that *Taiji Quan* was profound and infinitely variable.

2. Different Schools of *Taiji Quan*

In the original form of *Taiji Quan* there were leaps, stamping and bursts of sudden movement. At the start of the 19th century, a man from Yongnian County in Hebei Province, Yang Luchan, went to Wenxian County to work as a hired labourer in Chenjiagou Village, where he learned *Taiji Quan*. Later he returned to his home county and, because of his boxing skill, became known

---

*Metal, wood, water, fire and earth, held by ancient Chinese to compose the physical universe.

as "Yang the Invincible". Not long after, he was invited to the capital Beijing by the Qing imperial government to take up a post as a *wushu* instructor. *Taiji Quan* had now spread to the capital, and as it was developed by Yang and others in later years, it lost its fiercer movements, becoming softer, slower and more even. Hence, it became more suitable for practise by the old and the young, ideal as a health exercise.

As mentioned earlier, *Taiji Quan* has now developed into several different schools, the major ones of which are:

1) The Chen Style:

This is the original form from Henan developed by the Chen family. It did not reach Beijing until 1928. This style still retains some of the old jumps, stamps and bursts of strength, interweaving forceful and graceful movements. With many twists and turns, it is quite strenuous (Ill. 10).

2) The Yang Style:

Developed from the Chen style by Yang Luchan, its present form was developed by his grandson Yang Chengfu. It is currently the most popular style in China. Its movements are even and relaxed, with many wide arcs (Ill. 11).

3) The Wu Style:

Developed in Beijing by Wu Quanyou, a man of the Manchu nationality, and his son Wu Jianquan on the basis of their practice of the Yang style. Surpassed in popularity only by the Yang style, its movements are gentle, compact and unhurried, executed in arcs of a medium range (Ill. 12).

4) The Hao Style:

Originally developed by Wu Yuxiang, who studied

Ill. 10. Chen Xiaowang, the nineteenth-generation successor to the founder of the Chen-style *Taiji Quan*.

Ill. 11. Yang Zhenduo, successor to the founder of the Yang-style *Taiji Quan*.

Ill. 12. Wu Yinghua, successor to the founder of the Wu-style *Taiji Quan*.

Ill. 13. Yao Jizu, a master of the Wu-style *Taiji Quan*.

Ill. 14. Sun Jianyun, successor to the founder of the Sun-style *Taiji Quan*.

the Chen-style *Taiji Quan* in Henan. Wu's disciple, Hao Weizhen, brought it to Beijing. It is characterized by simplicity, clarity, and compactness, with soft and slow movements, their range small, and strict footwork and upright stances (Ill. 13).

5) The Sun Style:

At the end of the Qing Dynasty, Sun Lutang first studied *Xingyi Quan*, then *Bagua Quan*, and finally the Hao-style *Taiji Quan*, on the basis of which he developed his own style. Its movements are nimble, using fluctuations of open and closed hand methods. A distinct feature of the Sun style is its agile footwork, which advances and retreats nimbly (Ill. 14).

Despite their different methods, the above-mentioned five styles of *Taiji Quan* are similar in their basic routines.

Since the founding of the People's Republic, much effort has been made to promote *Taiji Quan* more widely. On the basis of the traditional styles, the physical culture and sports departments have re-edited and published the following new forms:

1) Simplified *Taiji Quan*:

Designed for the beginner, it is based on the Yang style, selecting the major movements combined into 24 forms. Its basics are easy to grasp.

2) 88-Move *Taiji Quan*:

Again based on the Yang style, it preserves the order of traditional *Taiji Quan*'s movements, while expressing the character of the Yang style in a more concentrated form.

3) Synthesized (66-Move) *Taiji Quan*:

Selected from the strong points of the various styles, it is fairly strenuous, suitable for those with some experience.

4) 48-Move *Taiji Quan*:

Also for the practitioner with some experience, it is again, based mainly on the Yang style, though incorporating features from some other styles. Lively, balanced and graceful, it breaks with the traditional order of movements.

3. Practice Methods

Taiji Quan's practice methods are essentially the same for each style, consisting of three main elements: individual practice, dual combat practice, and push-hands.

Most important and widely practised are the individual routines. The nature of these routines varies from style to style in length, complexity, strenuousness and speed.

Individual practice also includes single posture exercises, such as the 37 *Taiji* postures, which appeared some seventy years ago; the *Taiji* Internal Exercises, used today as a curative health exercise; the *Taiji* Standing Pole Exercise, and the *Taiji* Basic Skill Exercises.

Dual combat refers to practice of co-ordinated attack and defence and other combat skills according to a set pattern. They can be practised by two or more persons.

Push-hands is a style for practice or competition, used by each style of *Taiji Quan* as an exercise to develop reaction, combat skill and control.

There are also exercises with weapons, such as rapier, broad-sword, spear and staff, done either by individuals or by two people.

4. Basic Requirements in Practice

Despite the variations of each style, they all share the same basic requirements in practice.

1) Posture

Head: Naturally raised, without swaying or leaning to one side. Eyes level, mouth lightly closed, with tongue touching the upper palate.

Neck: Erect, but not tense, so that it remains flexible during practice.

Shoulders: Relaxed and sloping, never hunched up, pulled back or slumped forward.

Elbows: Always bent naturally and lowered. Avoid stiffness or raising them above the wrists.

Wrists: Relaxed, though never limp. Never bend them too far, so that the strength can flow easily to the hands.

Chest: Relaxed and slightly concave, never stuck out

or deliberately pulled in.

Back: Erect but relaxed, never bowed.

Waist: Held downwards and flexible, not pushed forward or stuck out backwards.

Backbone: Erect, so that the whole torso can naturally be held straight.

Buttocks: Tucked in slightly, not stuck out.

Hips: Straight, so that the strength can flow freely to the lower limbs; not twisted or sticking out.

Legs: Firm and solid, knees always slightly bent, flexible and free to turn and spin. Their movements smooth, light and stable, with weight distribution clearly distinguished.

2) Methods of Movement

Throughout the practice of *Taiji Quan* the body should remain relaxed and natural, never crooked or leaning. The mind leads the movements, which should be slow, smooth and light. They are executed in arcs or spirals, without any use of brute force, stiffness or fluctuations in speed. Though movements are agile and light, one must remain firmly rooted at all times, never losing one's centre. Co-ordination of the body is essential, and, where sudden bursts of strength are required, they must be quick without stiffness, the whole body moving as one.

Breathing should be natural and relaxed, allowing it to become smooth, deep and even. Movement and breathing should be co-ordinated, though breathing should never be forced for this purpose.

In combat, *Taiji Quan* emphasizes maintaining stillness and waiting for movement, reacting in response to the opponent's moves. One must control the opponent by complying with his oncoming force, seeking the latter's weak points and using a minimum of strength to overcome the larger force by skill and sensitivity. This requires a great deal of practice, developing sensitive awareness, accurate judgement, rapid reactions and great calm. In addition, one must develop strength to complement one's skill and combat awareness.

5. *Taiji Quan* and Health

Practice has increasingly improved the therapeutic value of *Taiji Quan*, and this is one of the reasons for its increasing popularity at home and abroad.

Training the mind and body at the same time, *Taiji Quan* exercises stimulate the brain, causing excitation in certain regions and protective inhibition in others. This enables the mind to rest, and relieves the brain of the pathological excitation caused by ailments, thus helping to cure some chronic diseases resulting from disorders of the nervous system.

In *Taiji Quan*, breathing is natural, sometimes involving abdominal respiration. It is thus effective in promoting respiration, blood circulation and digestion, gently stimulating the metabolism and self-regulating functions of the body. In addition, it has proved valuable in treating and preventing nervous disorders, heart disease, high blood pressure, pulmonary tuberculosis, tracheitis, ulcers and other chronic illnesses.

There are many cases of recovery from illness through the practice of *Taiji Quan*. An example is 55-year-old Xia Xiaoyu, who works at the China Children Publishing House in Beijing.

Previously, she was a liability at work, always suffering from illness. Over the years she had rheumarthritis, heart trouble and uterine bleeding. She was hospitalized eight times, but without any marked improvement. The doctor diagnosed her trouble as coronary heart disease. Once again, treatment saw no great improvement in her condition.

At the end of 1977, Xia Xiaoyu began to practise the 24-form simplified *Taiji Quan*. She found it difficult at first because she was so frail that she could not maintain one movement long enough to move smoothly onto the next. Nevertheless, she persevered, rising early each morning. After four years of practice, not only had her illnesses gone, but three years in a row she was able to take part in the Beijing old people's "New Long March" Sports Meet, winning a medal each time, including a gold medal. She became optimistic as never before. She was able to go to work as normal and do household chores without any problem. She was even able to go alone on business trips to other parts of China. While on an excursion to the Great Wall, she climbed to the highest point, on top of a signal tower. One could never have guessed that just a few years before she had been a veritable "medicine dispensary." Now, she and her daily practice of *Taiji Quan* are inseparable.

6. Illustrated Simplified *Taiji Quan* Exercise

Preparation posture:
Stand with the body naturally straight, neck erect, chin tucked in, feet close together, arms hanging down; mind concentrated, breathe naturally, eyes looking ahead (Fig. 1).

1) Starting Posture

a. Stand with feet apart as wide as the shoulders and toes pointing to the front (Fig. 2).

b. Slowly raise the arms to the front with the hands apart as wide as the shoulders and palms facing the ground (Fig. 3).

c. Raise the arms to shoulder level with fingers naturally bent and apart, and palms concave; wrists and elbows low, shoulders relaxed (Fig. 4).

d. Keep the upper body straight, slowly bend the knees to a half-squatting posture while pressing down lightly with palms (Fig. 5).

2) Mustang Parting Its Mane

a. Turn the upper body slightly to the right; bend the right arm horizontally to the front of the right chest with palm facing the ground; move the left hand to the chest, make an arc to the right and then down to the waist, the palm facing up as if holding a ball with both hands, eyes following the right hand (Fig. 6).

b. Move the body weight to the right leg, take the left foot to the inner side of the right foot, with toes slightly touching the ground (Fig. 7).

c. Turn the upper body slightly to the left, take a step forward to the left with the heel touching the ground; part the hands with one hand upwards to the left and the other downwards to the right (Fig. 8).

d. Bend the left knee with the right leg straight to make a left bow stance, keep turning the upper body while parting the two hands with the left hand to the upper left and the right to lower right until the left is raised in front of the eyes with the palm facing the forehead; put the right hand on the right hip, eyes following the left hand (Fig. 9).

e. Move the weight backwards, lift the left toe and turn to the left about 45 degrees (Fig. 10).

f. Turn the upper body slightly to the left, move the weight forward with hands in front of the left chest as if holding a ball with the left hand over the right one, eyes following the left hand (Fig. 11).

g. Take back the right foot to the inner side of the left foot with the toe lightly touching the ground or with the toe lifted when very skilled, eyes looking at the left hand (Fig. 12).

h. Take a step forward to the right with the right foot, heel touching the ground; part the hands, one raised to the upper right and the other lowered to the lower left, eyes looking at the right hand (Fig. 13).

i. Move the weight forwards, bend the right knee with the left leg straight to make a right bow stance; while turning the upper body to the right, part the hands to the upper right and lower left separately with elbows slightly bent, eyes looking at the right hand (Fig. 14).

j. The movements as shown in figures 15 to 19 are the same except that the left should be replaced by right, and *vice versa*.

3) The White Crane Spreading Its Wings

a. Turn the upper body to the left, turn the left hand over with the palm facing the ground, make an arc with the right hand to the front, palm facing up and left palm above facing down, as if holding a ball, eyes looking at the left hand (Fig. 20).

b. Take the right foot half a step forward to the back of the left foot with the front sole touching the ground (Fig. 21).

c. Move the weight backwards, turn the upper body to the right; part the hands slowly to the upper right and lower left separately, eyes looking at the right hand (Fig. 22).

d. Move the left foot forward slightly with the toe touching the ground and heel lifted off the ground; stop the right hand in front of the forehead on the right with the palm facing the left-rear; put the left hand on the left hip; eyes looking ahead (Fig. 23).

4) Holding the Knee in Bending Step

a. Turn the upper body slightly to the left, and at the same time, lower the right hand in front with palm up; lift the left hand slightly, eyes looking at the right hand (Fig. 24).

b. Turn the upper body to the right, move the right hand in an arc from the right side of the body to the side of the right hip, raise the left hand in front of the face, eyes looking at the left hand (Fig. 25).

c. Keep turning the upper body to the right, take the left foot to the inner side of the right foot with toes slightly touching the ground, while raising the right hand to the right-rear with palm up; lower the left hand to the front of the right chest with palm facing the ground, eyes looking at the right hand (Fig. 26).

d. Take the left foot forward to the left with the heel touching the ground while bending the right elbow until the right hand is higher than the right shoulder; lower the left hand to the front of the left hip (Fig. 27).

e. Bend the left knee with the front sole touching the ground and the right leg straight to make a left bow stance, turn the upper body to the left, push the right hand forward from the side of the right ear to the level of the nose, move the left hand in an arc passing the left knee and put the left hand on the left hip; eyes looking at the right hand (Fig. 28).

Fig. 1　　　　Fig. 2　　　　Fig. 3

Fig. 4　　　　Fig. 5　　　　Fig. 6

Fig. 7　　　　Fig. 8　　　　Fig. 9

Fig. 10   Fig. 11   Fig. 12

Fig. 13   Fig. 14   Fig. 15

Fig. 16   Fig. 17   Fig. 18

Fig. 19 Fig. 20 Fig. 21

Fig. 22 Fig. 23 Fig. 24

Fig. 25 Fig. 26 Fig. 27

Fig. 28

Fig. 29

Fig. 30

Fig. 31

Fig. 32

Fig. 33

112

f. Move the upper body backward and turn to the left with the left toe lifted and turned outwards (Fig. 29).

g. Put down the left toe and move the weight forward; keep turning the upper body to the left while raising the left hand to the left rear with palm up; lower the right hand to the front of the left chest, eyes looking at the left hand (Fig. 30).

h. Take the right foot to the inner side of the left foot with the right toe touching the ground (Fig. 31).

i. Move the right foot forward to the right with the heel touching the ground, bend the left elbow with the left hand higher than the left shoulder; put the right hand in front of the right hip (Fig. 32).

j. Move the weight forward, bend the right knee with the foot on the ground and the left leg straight to make a right bow stance; at the same time, turn the upper body to the right, push the left hand forward from the side of the left ear level with the nose; move the right hand by passing the front of the right knee before putting it on the right hip side, eyes looking at the left hand (Fig. 33).

k. All the movements from figures 34 to 38 are the same as those from figures 29 to 33 except that left should be replaced by right.

5) Swinging Pipa

a. Move the right foot half a step forward with the front sole touching the ground and land it at the back of the left foot (Fig. 39).

b. Shift the weight backward with the right heel touching the ground and the left heel slightly lifted; turn the upper body to the right; raise the left hand in front with fingers pointing upwards; draw the right hand back to the inner side of the left elbow, eyes looking at the left hand (Fig. 40).

c. Move the left foot slightly forward with the heel touching the ground and toe lifted, lower the elbows with the arms in arcs, hands level with the nose, the left palm facing right and the right hand facing the left elbow, eyes looking at the left hand (Fig. 41).

6) Upperarm Rolling

a. Turn over the hands with palms facing upwards, then put the right hand on the side of the right hip (Fig. 42).

b. Turn the upper body to the right, move the right hand backwards and upwards in an arc, eyes looking at the left hand (Fig. 43).

c. Lift the left foot; bend the right arm on the side of the right ear; lower the left arm, eyes looking at the left hand (Fig. 44).

d. Move the left foot backwards with the front sole touching the ground first and then the whole sole; move the weight backwards, with the front right sole touching the ground heel lifted off the ground push the right hand forward with the palm facing forward, take the left hand back to the stomach, eyes looking at the right hand (Fig. 45a-45b).

e. All the movements from figures 46 to 48b are the same as those from figures 43 to 45b except that the left should be replaced by right, and *vice versa*.

f. All the movements from figures 49 to 51b are the same as those from figures 43 to 45b.

g. For figures 46, 47 and 48a and 48b, refer to figures 52, 53 and 54a and 54b.

7) Pulling Peacock's Tail (Left)

a. Raise the right hand backward in an arc (Fig. 55).

b. Turn the upper body slightly to the right, bend the

Fig. 34

Fig. 35

Fig. 36

Fig. 37

Fig. 38

Fig. 39

Fig. 40

Fig. 41

Fig. 42

Fig. 43

Fig. 44

Fig. 45,1

Fig. 45,2

Fig. 46

116

Fig. 47

Fig. 48,1

Fig. 48,2

Fig. 49

Fig. 50

Fig. 51,1

Fig. 51,2

Fig. 52

Fig. 53

Fig. 54,1

Fig. 54,2

118

right arm to the front of the right chest; move the left arm downward in an arc, eyes looking at the right hand (Fig. 56).

c. Put the hands in front to make a "holding-ball" posture, left hand on the bottom, right hand on the top; move the left foot to the inner side of the right foot with toe touching the ground (Fig. 57).

d. Move the left foot forward with the heel touching the ground, toe lifted; part the hands upward to the left and downward to the right separately, eyes looking at the left hand (Fig. 58).

e. Move the weight forward, bend the left knee with the right leg straight to make a left bow stance, turn the upper body slightly to the left, push the left forearm forcefully forward with the hand at shoulder level; put the right hand on the right hip side, eyes looking at the left forearm (Fig. 59).

f. Stretch the right hand forward and upward under the inner side of the left elbow with the right palm facing upward and the left palm facing downward (Fig. 60).

g. Turn the upper body to the right with the weight moved back; pull the hands down from the stomach to the back, eyes looking at the right hand (Fig. 61).

h. Turn the upper body to the left, bend the right arm to the front with the right hand at the inner side of the left wrist, eyes looking at both hands (Fig. 62).

i. Bend the left knee with the right leg straight to make a left bow stance, push both hands from the chest forward with the arms bent, eyes following the left wrist (Fig. 63).

j. Part the hands to the left and right as wide as the shoulder with the palms facing the ground (Fig. 64).

Fig. 55 Fig. 56 Fig. 57

Fig. 58 Fig. 59

Fig. 60 Fig. 61

Fig. 62

Fig. 63

Fig. 64

Fig. 65

Fig. 66

Fig. 67

k. Tilt the upper body backwards; bend the right knee; lift the left toe; draw the hands to the chest (Fig. 65).

l. Keep tilting the upper body backward; put the hands in front of the stomach, eyes level (Fig. 66).

m. Move the body forward; put the weight on the left foot; bend the left knee with the right leg straight to make a left bow stance; push both hands forward with palms facing the front at shoulder level, eyes level (Fig. 67).

8) Pulling Peacock's Tail (Right)

a. Tilt the upper body backwards and turn it to the right, lifting the left toe (Fig. 68).

b. Keep turning the upper body to the right; turn the left toe inward; move the right hand in an even arc to the right, eyes following the right hand (Fig. 69).

c. Shift the weight to the left; move the right foot to the inner side of the left foot with toe touching the ground; put the right hand down with the palm facing upward; bend the left arm in front of the chest to make a "holding-ball" posture with the right hand underneath, eyes following the left hand (Fig. 70).

d. All the movements from figures 71 to 80 are the same as those from figures 58 to 67, except that left should be replaced by right.

9) Single Whip

a. Lean the upper body back and turn to the left; lift the right toe, lower the right hand slightly; move the right arm slightly to the left in an even arc, eyes following the left hand (Fig. 81).

b. Keep turning the body to the left with the left toe turned inward and touching the ground; both hands, with the left higher than the right, also turned to the left as the body turns; raise the left arm to the left with the

Fig. 68

Fig. 69

Fig. 70

Fig. 71

Fig. 72

Fig. 73

Fig. 74

Fig. 75

Fig. 76

Fig. 77

Fig. 78

Fig. 79

Fig. 80

palm facing left; raise the right hand from the front of the stomach to the side of the left rib, with the palm facing upward and eyes following the left hand (Fig. 82).

c. Shift the weight to the right leg; move the left foot close to the right foot with the toe touching the ground; move the right hand in an arc upward to the right and bend the right fingers close together with arms at shoulder level; move the left hand in an arc downward and then upwards to the right shoulder with the palm facing backward, eyes following the left hand (Fig. 83).

d. Turn the upper body slightly to the left; step with the left foot forward to the left with the toe turned outwards about 15 to 30 degrees and heel touching the ground; extend the left arm evenly to the left with eyes following the left hand (Fig. 84).

e. Move the upper body forward and turn to the left with the left front sole touching the ground; bend the left knee with the right leg straight to make a left bow stance, turn the left hand over and push forward, eyes following the left hand (Fig. 85).

10) Cloud Hand

a. Move the upper body backwards with the left toe lifted and the left hand lowered slightly (Fig. 86).

b. Move the upper body to the right, turn the left toes inward; move the left hand in an arc downward and to the right shoulder with the palm facing inward; eyes following the right hand (Fig. 87).

c. Turn the upper body to the left, move the right palm in an arc downward and to the stomach; move the left hand in an arc upward to the left shoulder with eyes following the left hand (Fig. 88-89).

d. Turn the left hand over gradually and move to the left in an arc with the palm facing the left; move the

Fig. 81

Fig. 82

Fig. 83

Fig. 84

Fig. 85

Fig. 86

Fig. 87

Fig. 88

Fig. 89

Fig. 90

Fig. 91

Fig. 92

127

Fig. 93

Fig. 94

Fig. 95

Fig. 96

Fig. 97

Fig. 98

Fig. 99

128

right hand in an arc from the stomach, upward to the left shoulder with the palm facing the body, move the right foot to the left with 10-20 cm between the feet, eyes following the left hand (Fig. 90).

e. Turn the upper body to the right, spread the right arm to the right in an arc; eyes following the right hand (Fig. 91).

f. Keep turning the upper body to the right, step with the left foot to the left with the front sole touching the ground first; turn the right hand outward gradually to the right side of the body; move the left hand in an arc from the stomach upward to the right shoulder with the palm facing upwards, eyes following the right hand (Fig. 92).

g. For the movements in figures 93 to 96, refer to figures 89 to 92.

h. For the movements in figures 97 to 99, refer to figures 93 to 95.

11) Single Whip

a. Turn the right hand over to the right and bend the fingers close together, move the right hand upward in an arc to the right shoulder with the palm facing the rear; lift the right heel, the eyes following the left hand (Fig. 100).

b. For the movements in figures 101 and 102, refer to figures 84 and 85.

12) Reigning the Horse

a. Move the right foot half a step forward behind the left foot, with the front sole touching the ground (Fig. 103).

b. Touch the ground with the left heel, lean back the upper body, lift the left heel; turn the hands over with palms facing upward (Fig. 104).

c. Move the left foot slightly forward with toe touching the ground, heel slightly lifted; turn the upper body to the left, push the right hand forward by the side of the right ear with the palm facing forward; move the left hand to the front of the body with the palm facing upwards, eyes following the right hand (Fig. 105).

13) Raising the Right Foot

a. Stretch the left hand to the right wrist with hands crossed (Fig. 106).

b. Move the left foot forward to the left with the heel touching the ground and toe lifted; part the hands to each side, eyes following the right hand (Fig. 107).

c. Move the body forward with the sole of the left foot touching the ground; keep the right leg straight to make a left bow stance, parting the hands to each side (Fig. 108).

d. Move the right foot to the inner side of the left foot with the toe touching the ground and heal lifted; cross the hands in front of the chest with the right hand behind the left hand and palms facing the chest, eyes looking ahead to the right (Fig. 109).

e. Bend the right knee; part the hands to each side, eyes looking at the right hand (Fig. 110).

f. Hold the arms on each side with elbows slightly bent and palms facing the front; raise the right leg with foot flexed (Fig. 111).

14) Twin Peaks

a. Bend the right knee; move the left hand from the rear in an arc forward to the front; turn the hands over with the palms facing upward and eyes looking at both hands (Fig. 112).

b. Put the right foot down in front to the right with the heel touching the ground; put the hands down from both sides of the right knee to the side of the hips (Fig. 113).

c. Put the right foot down with the front sole touching the ground; move the body forward, stretching the left leg to make a right bow stance; change the palms to fists and move them upward and forward to ear level with 10-20 cm between the fists and fist holes facing diagonally downwards, eyes looking ahead (Fig. 114).

15) Turning the Body and Raising the Left Foot

a. Move the body backward and turn to the left, lift the right toe and turn inward with the whole foot firmly on the ground; change the fists to palms and part to each side with eyes following the left hand (Figs. 115-116).

b. Move the body to the right and the left foot to the inner side of the right foot with the toe touching the ground; move the hands in arcs, first upward then downward in front of the chest, with palms facing the rear and eyes looking to the left (Figs. 117-118).

c. The movements in figures 119 and 120 are the same as those in figures 110 and 111 except that left should be replaced by right.

16) Standing on One Foot and Extending Left Leg

a. Take back the left foot with the knee bent, turn the upper body to the right and bend the right fingers. When turning the body, move the left hand in an arc to the right shoulder with eyes following the right hand (Fig. 121).

b. Bend the right knee and lower the body, extend the left leg to the left; move the left hand forward by the inner side of the left leg, with the palm facing forward and eyes following the left hand (Figs. 122-123).

Fig. 100

Fig. 101

Fig. 102

Fig. 103

Fig. 104

Fig. 105

132

Fig. 106   Fig. 107   Fig. 108

Fig. 109   Fig. 110   Fig. 111

Fig. 112   Fig. 113   Fig. 114

Fig. 115

Fig. 116

Fig. 117

Fig. 118

Fig. 119

Fig. 120

134

c. Move the body forward, bend the left knee with the right leg straight to make a left bow stance and raise the left hand; put the right hand down with fingers bent upward (Fig. 124).

d. Bend the right knee and lift it to the front with the toe pointing down; bend the left knee slightly, straighten the right fingers and swing the hand from the back forward by the right side of the leg and bend the elbow over the right knee with the palm facing to the left; put the left hand on the side of the left hip with the palm facing down and eyes following the right hand (Fig. 125).

17) Standing on One Foot and Extending the Right Foot

a. Put the right foot down on the right side of the left foot with the toe touching the ground, and turn the body to the left; move the left hand backward with fingers bent; move the right hand in an arc to the left shoulder with eyes following the left hand (Figs. 126-127).

b. Bend the left knee and lower the body, extend the right leg, put down the right hand and raise it by the inner side of the right leg, eyes following the right hand (Figs. 128-129).

c. The movements in figures 130 and 131 are the same as those in figures 124 and 125, except that left should be replaced by right.

18) Shuttling Back and Forth

a. Put down the left foot in the front with the toe pointing outward, turn the upper body to the left, put the hands in front of the chest with the right hand above the left as if holding a ball, eyes looking at the left forearm (Fig. 132).

b. Move the right foot to the inner side of the left foot

with toe touching the ground and step forward to the right about 45 degrees; straighten the left leg to make a right bow stance, move the upper body forward and turn to the right, raise the right hand and turn the palm over above the right forehead with the palm facing to the front, push the left hand downward and forward level to the nose, with the palm facing the front, eyes following the left hand (Figs. 133-135).

c. Move the upper body slightly back, turn the right toe outward, move the left foot to the inner side of the right foot with toe touching the ground; put down the right hand, spread the left hand in an arc to the right, put the hands in front, right hand above, left hand below as if holding a ball, eyes looking at the right hand (Figs. 136-137).

d. Step the left foot forward to the left (about 45 degrees) with the right leg straight to make a left bow stance, move the upper body forward and turn to the left, raise the left hand and turn over the palm above the left forehead with the palm facing upward; push the right hand backward to the right, down and forward, level with the nose, eyes looking at the right hand (Figs. 138-139).

19) Needle at the Bottom of the Sea

a. Take the right foot half a step forward with the toe touching the ground and put it at the back of the left foot; lift the left leg, turn the upper body to the right, put the left palm on the left knee; raise the right hand to the height of the right ear with the palm facing the left and eyes looking at the right hand (Figs. 140-141).

b. Put down the left foot with toes touching the ground and heel lifted; turn the upper body slightly to the left, stab the right hand down to the front; put the

Fig. 121

Fig. 122

Fig. 123

Fig. 124

Fig. 125

Fig. 126

137

Fig. 127

Fig. 128

Fig. 129

Fig. 130

Fig. 131

Fig. 132

Fig. 133

138

Fig. 134   Fig. 135   Fig. 136

Fig. 137   Fig. 138   Fig. 139

Fig. 140   Fig. 141   Fig. 142

left hand on the left hip, eyes looking on the ground in the front (Fig. 142).

20) Swinging the Back

a. Lift the left foot and both hands with the left palm facing down, fingers close to the right wrist and the right palm held sideways. (Fig. 143).

b. Put down the left foot in front with the right leg extended straight to the rear to make a left bow stance; move the body forward and turn to the right; put the right hand horizontally above the right forehead with the palm facing upward; push the left hand level with the nose, eyes following the left hand (Figs. 144-145).

21) Turning Body, Pulling, Blocking and Pounding

a. Lean the upper body back and turn to the right; move the right hand in an arc to the right; raise the left hand, eyes following the right hand (Fig. 146).

b. Move the body to the left and the right fist in an arc to the stomach, the fist facing down; raise the left hand in front of the left temple palm facing outward, eyes looking to the right (Figs. 147-147a).

c. Move the right foot back before placing it forward with the toe turned outward; turn the right fist outward from the front of the body with the fist upward, putting the left hand on the left hip with eyes following the right fist (Fig. 148).

d. Move the body forward and step forward with the left foot; stretch the left hand forward in an arc and block with the palm downward; put the right fist on the right hip with eyes following the left hand (Figs. 149-150).

e. Move the upper body forward, bending the left knee with the right leg straight to make a left bow stance; punch the right fist forward at the chest level; place the left hand at the inner side of the right forearm, eyes following the right fist (Fig. 151).

22) Stopping Blows

a. Stretch the left hand from under the right wrist with both palms facing upward; change the right fist to a palm with the palm facing upward, and hands apart as wide as the shoulders (Figs. 152-153).

b. Move the upper body backward, lifting the left toe; take the hands slowly back to the chest; turn the hands over and move to the front of the stomach with palms turned partly downward (Figs. 154-155).

c. Move the upper body forward, bending the left knee with the right leg straight to make a left bow stance; push the hands forward with the hands apart as wide as the shoulders, wrists at shoulder level, palms facing forward and eyes looking ahead (Figs. 156-157).

23) Crossed Hands

a. Move the upper body backward, turn to the right, and lift the left toe inward; turn the right toe outward, move the right hand with an even arc to the right with the left arm raised at the left side of the body and eyes following the right hand (Figs. 158-159).

b. Move the upper body to the left, turn the right toe inward, take the right foot to the left, at the same time moving the hands down to the stomach before raising them in arcs, and crossing in front with the right hand over the left and palms facing backward, eyes ahead (Figs. 160-162).

24) Finishing Posture

a. Turn the palms outward with palms facing downward, put them down on each side of the hips; eyes ahead (Figs. 163-165).

b. Move the left foot close to the right foot with the body naturally straight as in Preparation Posture (Fig. 166).

Fig. 143

Fig. 144

Fig. 145

Fig. 146

Fig. 147

Fig. 147

Fig. 148

Fig. 149

Fig. 150

Fig. 151

143

Fig. 152

Fig. 153

Fig. 154

Fig. 155

Fig. 156

Fig. 157

144

Fig. 158

Fig. 159

Fig. 160

Fig. 161

Fig. 162

Fig. 163

Fig. 164

Fig. 165

Fig. 166

III. *Shaolin Quan*

1. Shaolin Monastery and Shaolin *Wushu*

Shaolin Quan is one of China's most well-known traditional styles of *wushu*, its name originating from the Shaolin Monastery, an important centre in the development of Chinese martial arts (Ill. 15).

The monastery is situated in Henan Province, 13 kilometres northwest of Dengfeng County town at the western foot of Mt. Songshan. The name Shaolin comes from the fact that the monastery is nestled in the woods (*lin*) below the shady northen slope of Shaoshi Peak.

Shaolin Monastery was built in 495 under the patronage of Emperor Xiaowen (reigned 471-500) of the

Ill. 15. The main entrance to the Shaolin Monastery.

Northern Wei Dynasty, to accommodate a visiting Indian monk. During the 1,500 years of its history, it has gone through many ups and downs; at times a vast and thriving establishment, at others suffering decline and disaster.

In 573, Emperor Wudi (reigned 561-579) of the Northern Zhou Dynasty prohibited the Buddhist and Taoist religions. The Shaolin Monastery was abandoned. After 581, Emperor Wendi (reigned 581-605) of the Sui Dynasty revived Buddhism, granting the monastery 10,000 mu (666 hectares) of land and providing subsistence for the monks. Not long after, however, widespread uprisings and wars against the Sui resulted in the monastery being razed to the ground, with only a stone pagoda left standing.

By the reign of the Tang Dynasty Emperor Taizong (reigned 627-650), the monastery flourished once more, again in possession of more than 600 hectares of land, buildings with a total of more than 5,000 rooms, over 1,000 monks, and its own army and statutes.

In 1312, Emperor Renzong (reigned 1312-1321) of the Yuan Dynasty ennobled the abbot of the Shaolin Monastery as the Great Master of the Void and the Duke of Jin. However, at the end of the Yuan Dynasty, it met again with disaster, once more being consumed by fire. The buildings remaining today date from the Ming and Qing dynasties, and the title plaque, Shaolin Monastery, above the main entrance was written by Emperor Kangxi (reigned 1662-1723) of the Qing Dynasty. Unfortunately, its troubles were not yet over. In 1928, during a battle between feuding warlords, Shi Yousan sent troops to burn the monastary. The fire raged for more than 40 days, reducing most of the main halls to ashes and destroying many cultural relics.

After 1949, the People's Government put the Shaolin Monastery under protection and began repairing its buildings. Fully restored, it is now open to tourists.

Regarding the founder of *Shaolin Quan*, there has been much debate through the centuries. Tradition ascribes its beginnings to the Indian monk Bodhidharma who came to China and lived in the Shaolin Monastery early in the 6th century. Bodhidharma, it is said, developed a set of exercises for the monks to practise after their long periods of meditation, and these formed the basis of *Shaolin Quan*. However, though historians generally recognize that Bodhidharma was the founder of the Chan Sect of Chinese Buddhism, there is no evidence that he ever stayed in Shaolin Monastery for any length of time or that he knew anything about martial arts.

Historical material suggests that almost immediately after its founding, self-defence or some other form of physical training was part of life in the monastery. The account of Chan Master Zhou is interesting. It is said that when he entered the monastery as a weak boy he was often bullied, so he decided to learn martial arts, which made him physically tough and skilled in combat.

Whatever the origins of Shaolin *wushu*, by the end of the Sui Dynasty (581-618), the outstanding combat skills of the Shaolin monks became well known. At that time, Li Shimin, Prince of Qin, was leading his troops against his military rival, Wang Shichong at Luoyang. Li heard of the fighting skills of the Shaolin monks and called upon them to help him. The monks responded by capturing Wang's nephew, thus aiding the defeat of Wang and the founding of the Tang Dynasty by Li Shimin. Li rewarded the monks with titles, bestowing more land and privileges on their monastery and erecting a stele (an inscribed pillar) recording their achievements. The monastery precincts were expanded and the system of monk-soldiers was established. The fame of Shaolin *wushu* spread across China. The film *Shaolin Monastery*, was based on the story of the monk-soldiers who helped Li Shimin with their fighting skills.

From this time on, the monastery became a great centre for the development and practice of *wushu*. Practice became more varied: armed and unarmed skills, calvary and infantry combat were developed. Skilled *wushu* masters were frequently invited from all parts of China to teach the monks. For instance, the famous general of the Ming Dynasty, Yu Dayou, visited the monastery and taught them his staff skills. At the same time, the famed *wushu* master Cheng Chongdou came to learn Shaolin techniques, which began to spread wider.

Hence, many times in its history, the Shaolin Monastery became a focal point for *wushu*, assimilating what was best in the different schools of martial arts.

According to records, the *wushu* practised at the monastery in different periods was varied in style and content. Among the unarmed combat styles were those resembling the fast and agile *Chang Quan*. Others were powerful, like *Nan Quan*, or emphasized the use of will and the mind as well as breathing like *Xingyi Quan* (Will-Mind Boxing) and *Rou Quan* (Soft Boxing); still others imitated animal movements like *Luohan Quan* (Arhat Boxing) and *Hou Quan* (Monkey Boxing).

Shaolin staff skills were especially famous, although all the 18 military weapons were practised. In addition, many other forms of exercise evolved, such as the Standing Pole Exercise, Hard Skills, Light Skills and *Qi*

Ill. 16. Depression worn by practising *wushu* in the Thousand Buddha's Hall of Shaolin Monastery.

Gong (Breathing Exercise). Years of treading and stamping have worn depressions in the brick floor of the Shaolin Monastery's Hall of One Thousand Buddhas where the monks used to practise *wushu* (Ill. 16).

As the fame of Shaolin *wushu* spread, Shaolin monks received imperial summons to fight several times. They fought against Japanese pirates, who plundered the Chinese coast, wreaking havoc among the local people from the 14th century on, during the Ming Dynasty. Responding to an imperial call, Shaolin monks led by Yue Kong and Da Zaohua engaged the Japanese pirates in the area around present-day Shanghai. Records say that these monk soldiers fought bravely, wielding iron staffs. In one encounter, they relieved the seige on Shanghai. Later, however, they were all killed by Japanese pirates who lured them into an ambush.

Today, Shaolin Monastery and its *wushu* are as famous as ever, its varied, artistic styles proving popular at home and abroad.

2. Contents and Characteristics of *Shaolin Quan*

Shaolin Quan is an alternate name for traditional *Chang Quan*. It refers to a style which spread throughout China and is now regarded as one of the major components of *Chang Quan*. Its main skills are striking, kicking, throwing and manipulating. Its style can be summed up as fast, hard, agile and simple.

Fast—The movements should be quick. As the Shaolin sayings go, "The fist has form, but the strike seems formless," and "The movements are like the wind, and as agile as a monkey's."

Hard—Movements should be strong, but not stiff and inflexible.

Agile—Movements should never be predictable, but full of unexpected, yet smooth changes. Movements should not be obvious to the opponent in order to put him off guard and baffle him by feigning attacks. At the same time, movements should be nimble, not heavy and stiff. As the saying goes: "Elegant as a cat, fierce as a tiger, moving like a dragon, and standing fast as a nail."

Simple—Movements should be simple, without a complicated pattern of postures. A *Shaolin Quan* saying says: "The fist strikes along a line, straight to the target." Rising, descending, advancing, retreating, turning back and moving sideways should be powerful and simple, executed along one line and within the distance of two or three paces.

Shaolin Quan has spread widely across China. According to a rough estimate, there are more than 300 *Shaolin Quan* routines practised in China today. Well-known among these are *Dahong Quan* (Great Red Boxing); *Xiaohong Quan* (Lesser Red Boxing); *Luohan Quan* (Arhat Boxing); *Chaoyang Quan* (Turn-to-the-Sun Boxing), *Qinglong Chuhai Quan* (Dragon-Raising-from-the-Sea Boxing); *Babu Lianhuan Quan* (Eight Step Interlocking Boxing), *Jingang Quan* (Buddha's Warrior Attendant's Boxing), *Lianbu Quan* (Chain-Step Boxing), *Qixing Quan* (Seven-Star Boxing), *Meihua Quan* (Plum-Blossom Boxing), and *Pao Quan* (Cannon Boxing).

The range of movements, which use the larger muscles, makes *Shaolin Quan* an excellent excercise for every aspect of the physique, developing the muscles and flexibility and improving the functions of the internal organs. It also helps build will and stamina. At the same time, its movements are graceful, contributing to coordinated, elegant bearing.

The work of discovering, reorganizing and improving *Shaolin Quan* has received great attention from the People's Government. A spare-time *wushu* school has been established in Dengfeng County near the Shaolin Monastery, as well as a unit dedicated to researching the Shaolin tradition. They have collected self-defence manuals preserved among the people and discovered certain bare-hand and weapon routines. They have also trained *Shaolin Quan* teachers. Today, *Shaolin Quan* is spreading even more widely in China and many other countries.

3. Illustrated *Shaolin Tiangang Quan* (Heavenly Warrior Boxing)

Preparation posture: Stand straight with arms naturally hung by each side and eyes looking ahead (Fig. 1).

1) Showing the Palms with Light-Step Stance

a. Raise the left hand to the front and swing it to the right with the palm facing upward, and at the same time, lift the right hand to the hip with the palm facing upward, eyes following the left hand (Fig. 2).

b. Raise the right hand with the palm facing diagonally upward, and at the same time, lower the left hand, swing it to the left at shoulder level with fingers close together and pointing downward, eyes looking to the left (Fig. 3).

c. Swing the right hand to the left, downward and then to the right over the head, with the palm facing upward, and at the same time, move the left foot forward with toes touching the ground, eyes following the right hand and then look to the left. (Fig. 4).

2) Mustang Parting Its Mane (Holding Fists with Feet Together)

a. Step forward with the left foot while swinging the right hand to the right, down and to the front; swing the left hand to the front by passing the left side of the body, palms facing down and eyes ahead (Fig. 5).

b. Move the left foot half a step forward, and the right foot close to the left, and at the same time, raise the hands upward to each side and then to the back of the body with fingers close together pointing upward; look to the left (Fig. 6).

c. Stand still with fists on the hips, palms facing upward, look ahead (Fig. 7).

3) Fist to Fist

Stand still pushing the fists forward; move them downward to each side of the body and raise them upward; swing to the front and lower them to the front of the body at waist level, fist facing down, eyes looking left (Figs. 8-9).

4) Standing with One Foot (Stamping Foot and Holding Fists)

Turn the body to the left stretching the palms forward; swing to the left, change the palms to fists and then take them back to the hips with the palm side of the fist facing upward; at the same time, lift the right foot and stamp it forcefully on the ground, then lift the left knee with toe pointed; eyes ahead (Figs. 10-12).

Main points: Stamp the foot and pull the fists at the same time.

5) Pulling and Punching

Open the left fist, stretch the palm and then pull it back to the waist, and at the same time, move the left foot forward to make a left bow stance; punch forward with the right fist, eyes ahead (Figs. 13-14).

6) Striking from the Riding Stance

Move the left foot slightly backward with the heel pointing outward, and at the same time, turn the upper body to the right to make a riding stance; parry with the right fist, punch with the left fist to the left, the palm side of the fist facing forward, eyes looking to the left (Fig. 15).

7) Pressing the Elbows

Turn the body to the left, move the left foot slightly backward, heel lifted off the ground, turn the left fist outward and backward and press down; press the right fist down to the left with knuckles facing downward,

Fig. 1 Fig. 2 Fig. 3
Fig. 4 Fig. 5 Fig. 6
Fig. 7 Fig. 8 Fig. 9

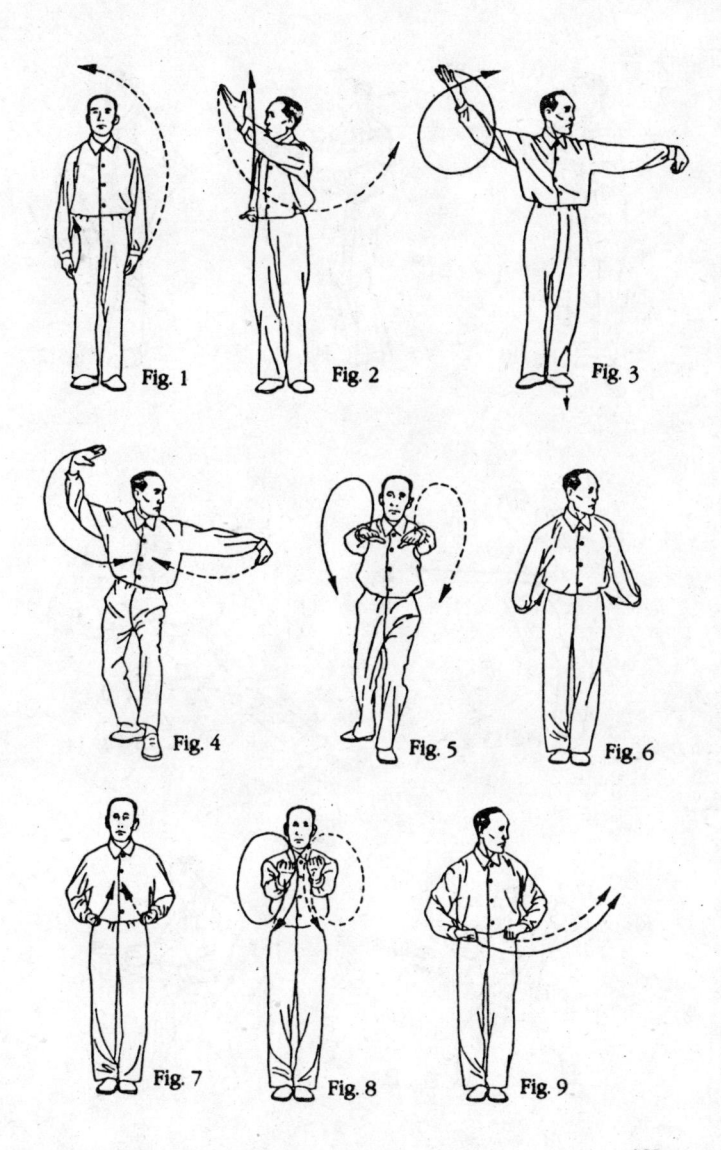

155

Fig. 10

Fig. 11

Fig. 12

Fig. 13

Fig. 14

Fig. 15

Fig. 16

eyes following the left fist (Fig. 16).

8) Punching with the Right Fist

a. Move the left foot forward with the toe pointing outward; put the fists on the waist, eyes ahead (Fig. 17).

b. Turn the body to the left, moving the right foot forward to make a riding stance; at the same time, raise the left fist over head and bend the elbow; punch with the right fist to the right, eyes looking to the right (Fig. 18).

9) Pulling and Pushing

a. Put the left foot behind the right foot with the front sole touching the ground; open the left fist to a palm, stretching foward from under the right forearm and upward to the right; open the right fist to a palm and pull it back to the right hip, eyes following the left palm (Fig. 19).

b. Turn the body slightly to the left, extending the right foot to the right and rear to make a left bow stance; close the left palm to a fist and pull it back to the hip with the fist hole facing upward; push the right palm swiftly forward, eyes following the right palm (Fig. 20).

Main points: Turn the body slightly to the right when putting the right foot behind the left one; move the foot backward simultaneously when pushing the hand.

10) Double Hand-Pushing

Move the left foot to the front of the right foot with the left leg slightly bent; kick with the right foot swiftly forward with the foot flexed, and at the same time, open the left fist to a palm; turn it and swing it to the left with the palm facing outward; lower the right palm and put it on the hip, eyes looking ahead to the right (Figs. 21-22).

11) Soaring Fist (Lifting the Knee and Stabbing the Fist)

Move the right foot to the right and lift the left leg, bending the knee with the toe pointed; close the right palm to a fist, pull it back to the waist, and stab with the right fist upward to the right with the fist facing diagonally upward; pull the left palm back under the right armpit and close the palm to a fist with eyes following the right fist (Figs. 23-24).

Main points: Bend the upper body slightly forward to the right, lifting the knee when stabbing the fist.

12) Palm Pushing

Turn the upper body slightly to the left, moving the left foot to the left with the right heel pointing outward to make a riding stance. At the same time, open the left fist to palm, and raise it from under the right arm to the left side of the forehead with the palm facing upward; open the right fist to a palm and push to the right from the waist, palm pointing diagonally upward and eyes following the right hand (Fig. 25).

13) Lifting Knee and Stabbing Palm

Turn the upper body slightly to the right; lift the left leg and bend the knee with the toe pointed and at the same time, swing the left arm in an arc to the right armpit and press the palm; thrust the right palm over the left forearm upward to the right, the palm facing upward and eyes following the right hand (Fig. 26).

Main points: Lift the knee simultaneously when thrusting the palm; the movement should be balanced and stable.

14) Turning Defeat into Victory

a. Turn the body swiftly to the left, move the left foot to the left to make a left bow stance, and at the same time, swing the right arm upward, to the left, downward and backward to the back of the body with fingers close together and pointing upward; swing the left arm upward to the left with the arm slightly bent and fingers pointing upward, eyes looking back to the right (Fig. 27).

b. Kick the right foot upward to the right with the foot flexed, eyes looking ahead (Fig 28).

c. Put the right foot down one step in front of the other, move three steps ahead in succession, eyes ahead (Figs. 29-32).

Main points: Move the feet with the waist low, the body stable, eyes following the left palm.

15) Turning the Body and Stretching

a. Turn the body to the right about 180 degrees with the left toe turned inward; move the right foot half a step backward to the right with toe turned outward, pulling back the left fist to the waist; gradually open the curved fingers into a palm and stretch forward while turning the body, eyes following the right hand (Fig. 33).

b. Put the left foot in front of the right, and the right behind the left, legs crossed and knees bent. At the same time, stretch the left fist from under the right forearm forward to the left with the palm side of the fist facing diagonally upward; pull back the right fist to the left side of the waist with eyes following the left fist (Fig. 34).

Main points: When swinging the right hand backward, curve the fingers forcefully. This movement should be done simultaneously with the movement of the right foot, and put the right foot behind the left when stretching the left fist.

16) Swinging and Punching

a. Lift the left leg and bend the knee while pulling the right fist back to the waist; turn the left forearm outward

Fig. 17

Fig. 18

Fig. 19

Fig. 20

Fig. 21

Fig. 22

Fig. 23

Fig. 24

Fig. 25

Fig. 26

Fig. 27

Fig. 28

Fig. 29

161

Fig. 30

Fig. 31

Fig. 32

Fig. 33

Fig. 34

Fig. 35

Fig. 36

and punch to the left with eyes following the left fist (Fig. 35).

b. Land the left foot to the left, turn the body to the left to make a left bow stance, swing the left fist downward, to the left and then over the head; punch forward with the right fist from the waist, eyes following the right fist (Fig. 36).

17) Magpie Landing on a Branch

a. Put the right foot behind the left, bend the knees, open the right fist to a palm and swing it upward to the right, downward, and to the front of the body; close the palm to a fist and punch the centre of the left palm; open the left fist to a palm, swing it to the left, downward, and to the front of the body, punching with the right fist, eyes looking to the left (Fig. 37).

b. Stand on the right leg, lift the left leg, bend the knee and kick to the left with toe bent inward. At the same time, open the right fist to a palm and swing it over head and to the left; curve the left hand when swinging the palm to the left side of the body, eyes looking to the left (Figs. 38-39).

Main points: Bend the body slightly to the right, while kicking to the side forcefully.

18) Rooster Standing on One Foot

Land the left foot beside the right; lift the right leg, and bend the knee with the foot flexed; swing the left arm downward, forward, upward, and backward on the right with fingers together and pointing upward; swing the right arm backward, downward, forward and upward with the fingers pointing upward and eyes following the right hand (Fig. 40).

19) Chopping with Extended Step

a. Turn the upper body to the left and swing the right

arm downward and to the left with the fingers pointing downward, and the eyes following the right palm (Fig. 41).

b. Jump with the left foot, turning the body in midair to the right about 180 degrees; land with the right foot first, and extend the left leg to the left to make an extended step; swing the arms upward, forward and chop downward with the palm centres facing each other and eyes looking down to the left (Figs. 42-43).

20) Kicking and Upward Shove

a. Shift the body weight to the left foot, flexing the right foot and kicking diagonally to the left. At the same time swing the arms upward over the kicking leg with palms facing forward, eyes ahead (Fig. 44).

21) Front Kicking

a. Move the right foot in front of the left and swing the arms backward and bend the wrists with fingers together and pointing upward, eyes looking ahead (Fig. 45).

b. Move the left foot one step forward; lift the right leg and bend the knee and kick forward with the foot flexed and eyes ahead (Fig. 46).

Main points: This can also be done when jumping in midair.

22) Bending the Knee and Stretching the Fist

Move the right foot in front of the left; lift the left leg and bend the knee, toe pointed and stretch the left fist upward to the right; stretch the right fist upward to the right from the waist, eyes following the right fist (Fig. 47).

23) Bending Elbow in Riding Stance

Move the left foot backward to the left to make a riding stance; open the left fist to a palm and swing it

Fig. 37

Fig. 38

Fig. 39

Fig. 40

Fig. 41

Fig. 42

Fig. 43

Fig. 44

Fig. 45

Fig. 46

Fig. 47

Fig. 48

Fig. 49

Fig. 50

to the left over the head with palm centre facing front; bend the right elbow in front of the chest and push the elbow to the right, eyes looking to the right (Fig. 48).

Main points: Move the foot and push the elbow simultaneously.

24) Rooster Standing on One Foot

a. Turn the upper body to the left while moving the left hand down and back with the fingers together and wrist bent; open the right fist to a palm and move it downward to the left, eyes looking back to the left (Fig. 49).

b. Keep turning the upper body and lift the left leg and bend the knee with the toe pointed. At the same time, turn the upper body to the right with the right hand swinging back and up to the right, and then back to the right and bend the wrist with fingers together and pointing upward; raise the palm upward with the fingers pointing upward, eyes following the left hand (Fig. 50).

Main points: Lift the leg and raise the hand simultaneously.

25) Bending the Right Elbow

a. Move the left foot to the left with toe slightly pointing outward and pull the right fist back to the waist; swing the left hand to the left, eyes following the left hand (Fig. 51).

b. Turn the body swiftly to the left and move the right foot forward to make a riding stance. At the same time, bend the right elbow and strike to the right; hold the right forearm with the left hand, looking to the right (Fig. 52).

26) Punching to the Right

Punch the right fist to the right from the waist;

change the left hand to a fist, raising it over head and bend the elbow with eyes looking to the right (Fig. 53).

27) Bending the Left Elbow

a. Turn the body to the right, moving the right foot half a step forward with toe pointing outward; pull the left fist back to the waist and punch with the right hand forward with hand curved, eyes following the right hand (Fig. 54).

b. Turn the body swiftly to the right, moving the left foot forward to make a riding stance. At the same time, bend the left elbow and strike to the left; hold the left forearm with the right hand, eyes looking to the left (Fig. 55).

28) Punching to the Left

Punch with the left fist to the left from the waist; change the right hand to a fist, raising it over the head and bend the elbow with eyes looking to the left (Fig. 56).

29) Double Punching to the Right

a. Move the upper body backward, pulling the left foot back with toe turned outward; pull the fists back to the waist with the thumb-side of the fist facing upward, eyes ahead (Fig. 57).

b. Move the right foot forward to make a right bow stance, and at the same time, punch with the fists to the right forcefully with the left fist over the head and the thumb-side of the fist facing down, and the right tumb-side of the fist, eyes looking to the right (Fig. 58).

30) Double Punching to the Left

a. Pull back the right foot with the toe turned outward. At the same time, pull the fists back to the waist with the knuckles facing down, eyes ahead (Fig. 59).

b. Move the left foot forward to make a left bow

stance; punch with the fists forcefully leftwards with the right fist over the head and the thumb-side of the fist facing down and the left fist with the thumb-side facing upward, eyes looking to the left (Fig. 60).

31) Chopping with Extended Step

a. Lift the left leg and bend the knee; pull the fists back to the waist with the palm side facing upward, eyes looking at the ground (Fig. 61).

b. Jump with the right foot and turn the body to the left while jumping; swing the hands upward opening the fists to palms (Fig. 62).

c. Land on the ground with the left heel, and at the same time, extend the right leg to the right; punch the left palm with the right hand, look to the right (Fig. 63).

Main points: Punch and extend the leg at the same time. Keep the waist low and the head raised.

32) Kicking in Midair

a. Bend the right knee with the left leg straight, and at the same time, swing the hands backward with wrists bent and eyes looking ahead (Fig. 64).

b. Lift the left leg and bend the knee; jump and kick the right leg forward with the foot flexed and the force of the movement going to the heel, eyes ahead (Fig. 65-66).

33) Lifting the Knee and Stretching

Land on the left foot first and then the right one; stab with the left hand from behind to the right; close the right palm to a fist and stretch forward over the left forearm to the right, with the palm side facing upward. At the same time, lift the left leg and bend the knee with the foot pointed, eyes following the right fist (Fig. 67).

Main points: Lift the knee at the same time as stretching the fist. The movement should be smooth and the upper body bent slightly forward.

34) Striking to the Right with the Riding Stance

Move the left foot to the left with the knees bent to make a riding stance; swing the left fist from under the right arm over the head and strike to the right with the right fist from the waist, eyes looking to the right (Fig. 68).

35) Striking with the Resting Step

Move the right foot behind the left with knees bent to make a resting step; swing the left fist to the right under the right elbow; pull the right fist back to the waist before striking to the right with the palm side of the fist facing upward, eyes following the right fist (Figs. 69-70).

36) Left Turn and Strike

a. Bend the left knee and the left leg, toe pointed; turn the upper body to the left while pulling the fists back to the waist, eyes looking at the ground (Fig. 71).

b. Put the left foot in front to the left, toe turned outward; move the right foot in front of the left to make a riding stance, at the same time, swinging the left fist down to the front and then raising it over the head; strike to the right with the right fist and the palm side of the fist facing upward, eyes following the right fist (Figs. 72-73).

37) Punching with the Resting Step

Move the left foot behind the right one with knees bent; raise the right fist, lower it down and pull it back to the waist; pull the left fist back to the waist, and strike forward forcefully with the palm side facing upward, eyes following the left fist (Figs. 74-75).

Fig. 51

Fig. 52

Fig. 53

Fig. 54

Fig. 55

Fig. 56

Fig. 57

Fig. 58

Fig. 59

Fig. 60

Fig. 61

Fig. 62

Fig. 63

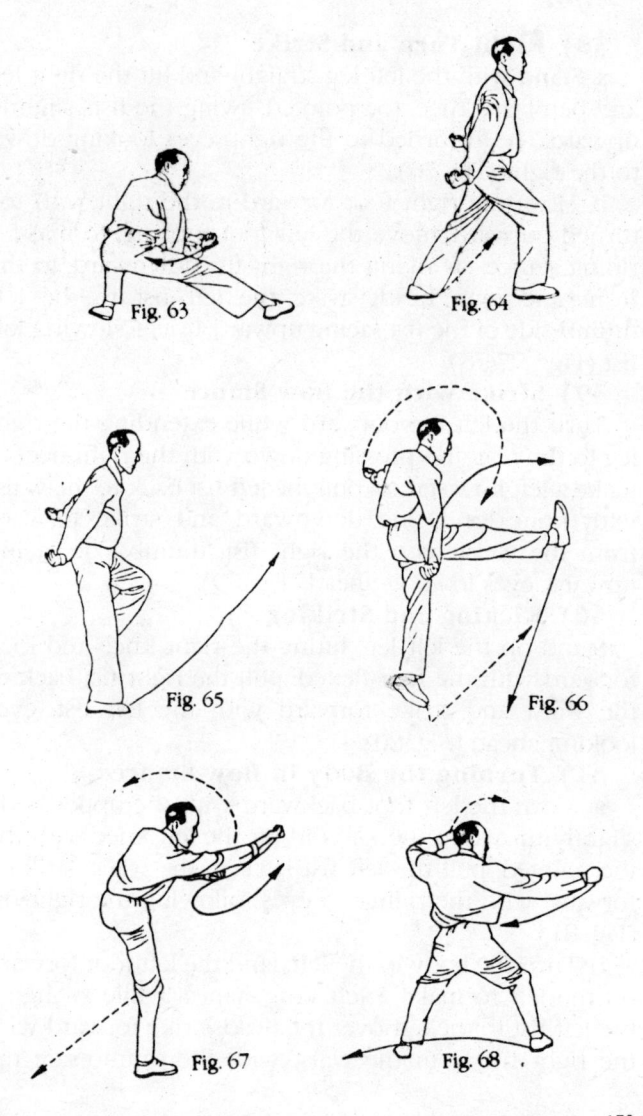

Fig. 64

Fig. 65

Fig. 66

Fig. 67

Fig. 68

38) Right Turn and Strike

a. Stand with the left leg straight and lift the right leg and bend the knee, toe pointed; swing the fists slightly upwards, head turned to the right, eyes looking down to the right (Fig. 76).

b. Move the right foot forward to the right with toe turned outward; move the left foot forward to make a riding stance, swinging the right fist downward, to the front and over head; strike the left fist to the left thumb-side of the fist facing upward, eyes following left fist (Figs. 77-78).

39) Strike with the Bow Stance

Turn the left toe outward while extending the right leg to the rear and pressing down with the right heel to make a left bow stance; pull the left fist back to the waist with knuckles facing downward and strike forward from the waist with the right fist, thumb side facing upward, eyes looking ahead (Fig. 79).

40) Kicking and Striking

Stand on the left leg, lifting the right knee and kick forward with the foot flexed; pull the right fist back to the waist and strike forward with the left fist, eyes looking ahead (Fig. 80).

41) Turning the Body in Bow Stance

a. Move the left foot backward with the upper body slightly turned to the left and lift the left knee with the toe pointed; pull the left fist back to the waist, striking forward with the right fist, eyes following the right fist (Fig. 81).

b. Turn the body to the left, land the left foot forward on the left to make a left bow stance, while swinging the left fist to the left over the head; strike forward with the right fist from the waist with the thumb-side up,

Fig. 69

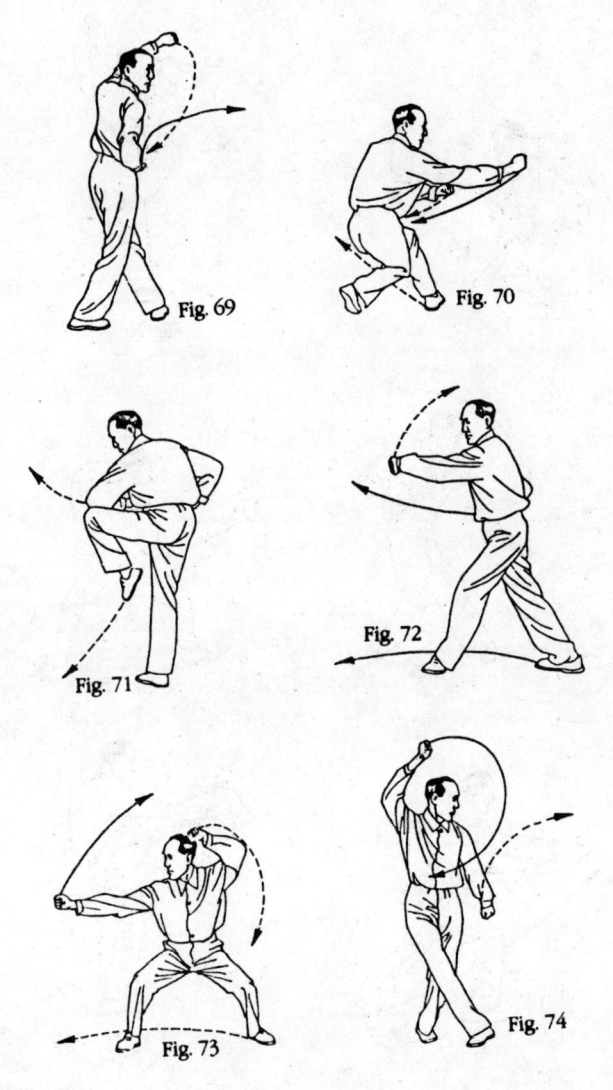

Fig. 70

Fig. 71

Fig. 72

Fig. 73

Fig. 74

175

Fig. 75

Fig. 76

Fig. 77

Fig. 78

Fig. 79

Fig. 80

Fig. 81

Fig. 82

Fig. 83

Fig. 84

Fig. 85

Fig. 86

eyes ahead (Fig. 82).

42) Leg Swing

a. Turn the body to the right, lifting the right knee with the toe pointed, while swinging the hands on each side of the body with wrists bent backward, eyes looking ahead to the right (Fig. 83).

b. Keep the upper body as it is, swinging the right leg from the left to the right with foot flexed (Fig. 84).

43) Fist to Fist

a. Land the right foot ahead on the right side and move the left foot close to the right; close the hands to fists and swing them downwards, to the front of the chest with fists facing each other and downward, eyes looking to the left (Fig. 85).

Finishing posture: Arms hang naturally at each side, eyes looking ahead (Fig. 86).

图书在版编目(CIP)数据

中国武术指南:英文/李天骥,杜希廉著.
—北京:外文出版社,1995
(传统体育)
ISBN 7-119-01393-9

Ⅰ.中… Ⅱ.①李… ②杜… Ⅲ.武术—中国—指南—英文
Ⅳ.G852-62

中国版本图书馆 CIP 数据核字(95)第 13853 号

中国武术指南

李天骥　杜希廉　编著

*

ⓒ外文出版社
外文出版社出版
(中国北京百万庄路 24 号)
邮政编码 100037
中国科学院印刷厂印刷
中国国际图书贸易总公司发行
(中国北京车公庄西路 35 号)
北京邮政信箱第 399 号　邮政编码 100044
1991 年(34 开)第一版
1995 年第二次印刷
(英)
ISBN 7-119-01393-9 /G·30(外)
01650
7-E-2377P